www.wadsworth.com

wadsworth.com is the World Wide Web site
for Wadsworth and is your direct source to
dozens of online resources.

At *wadsworth.com* you can find out about
supplements, demonstration software, and
student resources. You can also send email
to many of our authors and preview new
publications and exciting new technologies.

wadsworth.com
Changing the way the world learns®

THE ACTOR'S CHECKLIST

CREATING THE COMPLETE CHARACTER

Second Edition

ROSARY O'NEILL
Loyola University

WADSWORTH
™
THOMSON LEARNING

Australia • Canada • Mexico • Singapore • Spain
United Kingdom • United States

WADSWORTH

THOMSON LEARNING

Theatre Editor: Holly J. Allen
Assistant Editor: Cydney Erickson-Feinstein
Editorial Assistant: Mele Alusa
Marketing Manager: Kimberly Russell
Marketing Assistant: Neena Chandra
Advertising Project Manager: Shemika Britt
Project Manager, Editorial Production:
    Angela Williams Urquhart
Print/Media Buyer: Jessica Reed

Permissions Editor: Marcy Lunetta
Production Service: G&S Typesetters
Text Designer: G&S Typesetters
Copy Editor: Mike Nichols
Cover Designer: Beverly Baker
Cover Image: Photodisc © 2002
Compositor: G&S Typesetters
Printer: Transcontinental Printing, Louiseville, Quebec

Printed in Canada
1 2 3 4 5 6 7 05 04 03 02 01

For more information about our products, contact us at:
Thomson Learning Academic Resource Center
1-800-423-0563

For permission to use material from this text, contact us by:
Phone: 1-800-730-2214
Fax: 1-800-730-2215
Web: http://www.thomsonrights.com

Asia
Thomson Learning
60 Albert Street, #15-01
Albert Complex
Singapore 189969

Australia
Nelson Thomson Learning
102 Dodds Street
South Melbourne, Victoria 3205
Australia

Canada
Nelson Thomson Learning
1120 Birchmount Road
Toronto, Ontario M1K 5G4
Canada

Europe/Middle East/Africa
Thomson Learning
Berkshire House
168-173 High Holborn
London WC1 V7AA
United Kingdom

Latin America
Thomson Learning
Seneca, 53
Colonia Polanco
11560 Mexico D.F.
Mexico

Spain
Paraninfo Thomson Learning
Calle/Magallanes, 25
28015 Madrid, Spain

Library of Congress Cataloging-in-Publication Data
O'Neill, Rosary.
    The actor's checklist : creating the complete character / Rosary O'Neill.— 2nd ed.
        p. cm.
    Includes bibliographical references.
    ISBN 0-15-506105-4 (pbk.)
    1. Acting   I. Title.

PN2061 .O54 2002
792′.028—dc21

2001055934

This book is dedicated to
actors, the bravest people I know;
my children—Rachelle, Barret,
Rory, and Dale—who shared me;
my students, who encouraged me;
and my enthusiastic editor, John Swanson,
and his assistant Melinda Bonnell, both of
whom believed in me.
Bravo!

———————————

BRIEF CONTENTS

Preface   xiii
Introduction   xv

1 ACTION   1

2 OBJECTIVE   21

3 OBSTACLES   43

4 INNER IMAGES   61

5 THE SCORE   75

6 CHARACTER   97

7 SETTING   121

8 GIVEN CIRCUMSTANCES   149

APPENDIX A   175

APPENDIX B   177

APPENDIX C   179

APPENDIX D   183

Reading List   185
Credits   189

DETAILED CONTENTS

Preface   xiii
Introduction   xv

1 ACTION   1

What Is an Action?   1
Finding Action in Scripts   8
Rehearsals   10
Improvisation   15
Checklist   16
Final Projects   16

2 OBJECTIVE   21

What Is an Objective?   21
Opposing Objectives   26
Objectives in Each Relationship   31
Rehearsing Objectives   34
Checklist   38
Final Projects   38

3 OBSTACLES   43

What Is an Obstacle?   43
Discovering Obstacles   48
Rehearsing Obstacles   57
Checklist   59
Final Projects   59

4 INNER IMAGES   61

What Is an Inner Image?   61
Sending Inner Images   69
Checklist   71
Final Projects   72

5 THE SCORE   75

What Is a Score?   75
Finding the Elements   77
Scoring and Rehearsing   84
Checklist   93
Final Projects   94

6 CHARACTER   97

What Is Character?   97
Observation   98
Character Analysis   99
Physical Traits   100
Psychological Traits   105
Checklist   110
What Is a History?   110
What Is a Life Script?   113
Discovering the History   114
Writing the Biography   116
Checklist   117
Final Projects   117

7 SETTING   121

What Is the Setting?   121
The Time   122
The Place   135
Objects   137
Atmosphere   143
Checklist   145
Final Projects   145

8 GIVEN CIRCUMSTANCES   149

What Are Given Circumstances?   149
The Scene Breakdown   153
Background   165

Final Remarks   169
Checklist   171
Final Projects   171

**APPENDIX A IMPROVISATIONS,
GAMES, EXERCISES   175**

APPENDIX B KEY TERMS   177

APPENDIX C SCENE SELECTIONS   179

Man-Woman Scenes   179
Woman-Woman Scenes   180
Man-Man Scenes   181

APPENDIX D MONOLOGUE SELECTIONS   183

Women   183
Men   184

Reading List   185
Credits   189

PREFACE

Acting is a time-honored art. The oral tradition has been handed down for years and the written tradition has flourished in this century. The Russian master Constantin Stanislavski revolutionized the teaching of acting when he formalized the "hands-on" process. This book examines eight of the principles he clarified and presents them for your understanding today.

The book provides techniques for use in both classroom and production situations. Primarily intended for an initial acting course, the book will provide a resource when you begin to operate completely on your own. It should serve as a guide to your expressiveness onstage.

My understanding of these principles has been enhanced by interaction with over one hundred artists across America and Europe. Much of the study was conducted while rehearsals and performances were in progress. I have implemented these ideas with my students in New Orleans and with members of my professional theater company at Southern Rep, a state theater of Louisiana. This book has been classroom tested over a period of fifteen years. The eight chapters can be taught in a sixteen-week semester, allowing two weeks for the implementation of exercises in each chapter.

I want to thank Maria Mason, director of actor training for Southern Rep and adjunct professor at Tulane University, and my colleagues Dale Edmonds and Paul Schierhorn.

I would also like to thank the many helpful reviewers for their comments during the review process. Other individuals who deserve thanks include Denise Gremillion, Jose Rodriguez, and Lesley Schilling.

Thomson Learning provided essential assistance throughout the preparation of the final manuscript. Thanks are due to Angela Williams Urquhart, Cathy Linberg, and Jessica Reed.

I want to thank my acquisitions editor, John Swanson, for his determined support, his assistant Melinda Bonnell for her insightful guidance, and Gretchen Otto, Production Coordinator. They believed in the worth of this book and saw the revision through to completion. For the thorough advice of these three individuals and the leadership of David Tatom, I am grateful. I would also like to thank my true friend, Bob Harzinski.

Rosary O'Neill
New Orleans, 2001

INTRODUCTION

Acting is a daring art. An actor walks out nightly before an audience of strangers and expresses himself fully in public. His knees may be weak, but the audience sees only what the trained actor wishes it to see.

As you study acting you will gain more poise; you will learn how to appear comfortable in the most stressful of situations. Notice how your personality expands because of your increased creativity. Acting frees you to open yourself up, to try new things, to relate to all sorts of situations and people.

One recent study of corporate America claims that a person's rise to success is in direct proportion to his or her sense of audience. By studying acting you will learn to trust your impulses; you will know how to read between the lines; you will acquire the ability to relate to people with whom you have nothing in common. The skills you learn as an actor will help you complete your first job interview, present a new product line to a group of conservative investors, get the person of your dreams to date you.

Although based in the teachings of the great acting teacher Constantin Stanislavski, this book includes insights by other famous acting teachers, such as Uta Hagen, Sanford Meisner, Lee Strasberg, Michael Chekhov, and Stella Adler, integrated with Carl Jung's theories for tapping the unconscious. Of course, it is also based on what I have learned in my twenty years' experience as an actress, acting teacher, director, playwright, and founding artistic director of Southern Rep, a state theater of Louisiana.

You must practice to be successful at anything you do in life. This book provides you with a checklist of eight techniques used to inspire strong performances. Practice them, commit them to memory; with them you will build a solid foundation so that someday, either onstage or off, you will rivet your audience.

1

ACTION
What am I doing?

This chapter deals with what you do physically.
Each beat is composed of a unit of similar actions.

As I grow older, I pay less attention to what men say. I just watch what they do.

Andrew Carnegie

■ WHAT IS AN ACTION?

Why is action the chief element?

This book outlines the essential checklist for an actor to create a riveting performance. Aristotle in fifth-century Athens said drama is the imitation of action. And that definition holds true today. More than any other principle, action holds the key to any role. Acting means doing. We understand a story by what the actors do onstage. To act is to do. Remember a pivotal moment in your life: a wedding, a funeral, a graduation. Don't you see yourself in action doing something: parading down the aisle, throwing a rose on the casket, accepting the diploma? Yes, you may say, but what you were feeling was more important than the action. But the observer understands that feeling through action: the way you ran down the aisle, threw the rose, grabbed the diploma.

We can never disconnect our physical actions from our inner motivations. As long as we are alive, we'll think, feel, move. Our emotional, intellectual, and physical selves are interconnected. Death ends action. When we rehearse what we are doing on-stage, we are always assessing what we are thinking or feeling. But we capture thought and feeling through physical action. Thought and emotion are volatile, butterfly-like, hard to grasp and re-create. Physical action can be specified and repeated. What we do stirs up and is stirred up by thoughts and feelings. The key principle of acting is *to play action* in each beat of the script.

What is a beat?

Some say the term *beat* comes from the Russian pronunciation of *bit*, because disciples of Stanislavski spent countless hours exploring each bit of a scene. A beat is a slice of a scene with the same ingredients. It is the smallest unit of conflict. Sequences of beats create the pyramid of dramatic action. Each character confronts conflict in a series of beats that creates the scenes, the acts, and the play.

You must break down the material in each scene into interesting beats. Your interpretation results from how you shape these units. The script is your blueprint. No character is play-proof. You base your choices for the beats on information discovered in the text. "Working moment to moment" is a phrase actors use to describe a method for discovering each beat of the text.

What things make up a beat?

In a beat, you are looking for four elements: an action (something to do), an objective (something to want), an obstacle (something to overcome), and an inner image (something to motivate). These elements stimulate the tension in each beat. You probably already call upon some of them instinctually, because they are based on your normal reactions as a human being. In the next several chapters, we'll study these elements.

Action = "to do"

Action means "to do." Onstage, you are always engaged in action. A beat or small piece of a scene is primarily a sequence of similar actions. Your life is also composed of sequences of action. Some days the sequences are vivid. Imagine some of the highlights from your life: receiving a graduation diploma, reciting your wedding vows, embracing a dying friend. You have experienced more moving episodes or beats than you'll ever play onstage.

How do I name actions?

Onstage, you must identify the action you're playing. Because acting is doing, you are looking for verbs that capture inner and outer movements, verbs that stimulate thought and activity. You name action in an attempt to clarify (and thus repeat) the instinctual choices you make onstage. By choosing clear verbs, you pinpoint the distinctions in choices. "To badger" differs from "to irritate." The range of colors in your performance depends on your ability to identify and re-create many shades of action. In one sequence, you might use all these actions when flirting: "to coo, to toy, to expose, to tease, to humor, to entice, to tempt, to giggle."

To name actions, use the infinitive form of an active verb. For example, for the action "to wait," use the active verb "to amuse myself." It forces you to discover what you're doing, whereas "to wait" encourages passivity. When rehearsing actions, jot down verbs you are playing: "to punish, to ignore, to attack, to distract," and so forth. At home, find other verbs to experiment with in rehearsals. Succinct terms like "to dump him" work better than lengthy descriptions like "to get this person out of my life."

You follow impulses to discover actions in rehearsal. The more you understand what you're doing, the more actions may come to mind. By naming action, you clarify what you did so that you can do it again. Precision and detail are encouraged through such experimentation.

A thesaurus can help you clarify what you're doing. Use verbs like "to con" or "to slug" that evoke an emotional response in you. Study books on human behavior. Psychology books like Eric Berne's *Games People Play* can reveal the manipulating action of a scene. Your character may be engineering a game "to get revenge," as in "Now I've got you, you son of a bitch!" or to "show off," as in "Look, Ma, no hands!" or "to blame," as in "See what you made me do!" The library and other people can help you.

Remember, action that can be put into words and repeated is yours. Homework that reviews and strengthens what you do in rehearsal can help your subconscious store it. In performance, when you know what you're doing, you play free. You simply react to what is given to you moment to moment.

What is psycho-physical action?

Onstage, you'll be looking for physical and psychological action. Your physical action is what you do with your body. Your psychological action is what you think. But all action is psycho-physical. You can't separate your thoughts from your body. Although some actions are more physical than others, all have a psychological component. For example, the physical action "to slug the robber" will have some psychological factors affecting it. Oftentimes action is misinterpreted as purely movement around the stage, but really action has more to do with inner movement like "to get revenge" as it is expressed in your stage choices. So when choosing action, imagine what your character is thinking, experiencing. How does her body feel? What is she sensing? What images are stirring up her thoughts?

Nearly all stage actions are psychological, that is, they express your character's thoughts. Your character is constantly performing mental activities such as judging, envying, resenting, evaluating, repenting, worrying. Human beings are thinking machines. You spend much of your time assessing things. You can stop walking, but you can't stop thinking. Try right now, for one minute, to stop assessing things. It's impossible.

How do I physicalize an action?

To *physicalize* means to find the outward, physical expression of the internal, psychological action. Often a psychological action will have a completely physical expression. If your psychological action is "to punish someone," you might attempt to slap him. If your action is "to flirt," you might adjust your friend's collar. Look for different ways to relate psychological action to the body. In the balcony scene of Shakespeare's *Romeo and Juliet*, Romeo woos Juliet with his words. The actor might perform several physical activities while speaking, such as leaping the wall, throwing a rose to Juliet, staring at her, or caressing her cheek. For instance, Romeo could rush toward Juliet when saying "For stony limits cannot hold love out," because the line's action demonstrates the power of love (act 2, scene 2, line 67).

Active choices urge you to do something physical with the line. Imagine a scene in which you have to apologize to someone so he'll forgive you. If the text says, "I'm terribly sorry," you could just speak the words, but then you're not acting. In acting, you actively engage in behavior that communicates the remorse. For instance, you could drop to your knees or sob when you say the line.

Remember, you can concentrate on only one action at a time. If you play two actions, you must choose which is predominant. The lesser action becomes an activity. An activity is a task you do while engaged in the primary action. For example, think of the difference between an eating scene where the main action is "to gobble down your food" and one in which the action is "to seduce." In the latter example, eating becomes an activity.

Why is using a physical task important?

Because the audience can't tell what you're thinking, an activity or task helps you express your thoughts. For instance, you can suggest erotic thoughts by the way you handle your food. Find timely tasks that stir your emotions. If your action is "to withdraw," and it is appropriate, you could be packing. Imagine the thoughts, feelings, sensations tied to the way you deal with certain objects: a new résumé, a wedding ring, a plane ticket, a passport. If you're packing, are you worried about making the flight, about meeting someone, about leaving home? Later on, in scripted work, certain tasks, clothes, and objects may be specified by the playwright.

Clothing and objects can help you physicalize your actions. If your action is "to interview for a job," your attire will influence your action. If you are dressed in a dirty jacket and sweaty gloves, your actions will be different from those you perform when in a pristine pinstripe suit.

Why are physical actions important?

Stanislavski discovered that through physical actions, actors tap into psychological actions. By grounding you in the reality of the scene, physical actions help you focus your thoughts.

Climactic scenes, such as that of Oedipus pulling out his eyes, revolve around physical action. In the latter part of his life, Stanislavski concentrated on physical actions as the road to emotional involvement. Whenever possible, he encouraged playing them in order to galvanize the actor's sense of moment-to-moment reality.

Stanislavski stressed physical actions because they communicate immediately with an audience and simultaneously create the actor's sense of reality. They encourage both actor and audience to believe what is occurring onstage. For example, if you want to get across the idea that you want desperately to recover from an illness, you may succeed with a physical action like meticulously taking your temperature every five minutes.

Why do I need stamina?

Stamina will help you sustain a range of actions so you can behave imaginatively in whatever role you play. A change of voice, a tilt of the head, a shift in the gait—all require physical dexterity. Stamina encourages you to act in quick rhythm and tempo and to respond sharply to the other actors.

For any interpretation, you play hundreds of actions. Learn to recognize the demands being placed on your body and voice. Some actions require training in combat techniques, whereas others require vocal adjustments. Even when portraying a wounded character, you must project the incapacitation to the audience through your trained body and voice. A full year before he tackled Shakespeare's military hero Othello, Laurence Olivier went into daily training, running track and vocalizing his lower voice. Of all of the qualities necessary for actors—talent, training, stamina—Olivier placed stamina first. Even in his eighties, he swam sixty laps a day. Actors know that being in shape gives you an edge in performing action. Great actors are often fanatics about the human body.

EXERCISES

1. *Objects on a Tray.* Actors have two minutes to observe twenty-five diverse objects placed on a tray, then two minutes to jot down all the objects remembered. Action: to remember more objects than anyone else.

2. *Grocery Store.* Sit in a circle. One actor begins, "I packed my bag for Grandmother's house, and in it I put an *a* (apple)." The next actor repeats all that went before and inserts a *b* item. The next actor adds a *c* item, and so forth. An actor who forgets or mistakes an item is eliminated from the circle. Action: to list the most objects.

3. *Number Shoot.* Sit in a circle. Count off around the circle, with each actor taking a number. Then Actor Number One calls out, "One says to Three." Actor Number Three might

respond, "Three says to Eight." Then Eight responds with something like "Eight says to Four." An actor is put out of the circle if she does not respond immediately to her number or calls upon an incorrect number (the number that was just called or the number of an actor already eliminated). Action: to call the correct number.

4. *Unrelated Activity.* Do a complex task—fixing a radio, making a soufflé, manicuring your nails. Re-create precisely all the steps in the activity. Next, find a monologue totally unrelated to the activity. Identify the main action in the monologue and practice it separately. Next, do the monologue while performing the task. (Note: Just put the monologue to the activity and see how a physical task empowers action.)

■ FINDING ACTION IN SCRIPTS

How do I develop a range of actions?

You develop a range of actions by breaking down the scene. Begin by choosing your character's actions in each beat. Actions should be clear, creating something the audience can see. Naming what you're doing helps you distinguish and sustain interesting choices. Note how one actor has named the actions in the following beat.

BEAT 1: SLIPPING ONTO THE BUS

Scene: a bus in New Orleans

Major action: to slip by the bus driver
ACTIONS

1. to hurry onto the bus
2. to slug change into the fare box
3. to look for twenty more cents
4. to scramble inside my bag

5. to dump out my wallet

6. to moan

7. to rub my back

8. to check my pockets

9. to wave my eviction notice

10. to droop my shoulders

11. to ransack my bag for change

12. to slam more change into the box

13. to knife the driver with a dirty look

14. to stride down the aisle

In this beat, all the actions are related but *varied.* To keep audience interest, never repeat actions unless that repetition makes an important dramatic point. Your goal is to reveal your character through actions that are both exciting and fresh.

How do I extend my range in a beat?

You extend range by how you view your character. When in doubt, lean your interpretation toward the strong action coming from the strong trait: acting madly in love rather than sort of attracted, brokenhearted rather than hurt, furious rather than upset. These extremes of character inspire the peaks of your action and allow for moderate choices in between because it's easier to tone down a choice than to bolster it up.

When a script emphasizes one character action, you can extend your range by implementing an opposing one. For example, if you are playing an icy spinster, look for the moments when she is warm. Play her passionate when she says, "I'm perfectly calm, Mrs. Falk." Give your choice the benefit of complexity. Look for your character's opposing emotional traits. In *My Life in Art,* Stanislavski said: "Understand, I said to one of them, you are playing a hypochondriac. You are nagging all the time, and seemingly take care only that your part might, God forbid, not be that of a hypochondriac. But why worry about it when the author himself has taken care of it already? When you play a good man, look for the places where he is evil, and in an evil man look for the places where he is good."

Discover opposing actions by studying the play. Some roles, such as a messenger, for instance, may be vaguely written. Add your own imaginative characterization. Small roles sometimes present an opportunity for testing outrageous actions, like those of a "playboy," "rock singer," or "astronaut." Because you may resist negative actions, phrase actions in an enticing way. In life, you excuse distasteful actions. You see yourself as determined, not bullheaded; as carefree, not sloppy; as fun-loving, not foolish; as harried, not negligent. Onstage, play the positive. Interpret the character so positively that even repulsive actions seem natural.

■ REHEARSALS

How do I discover my actions in rehearsals?

In rehearsals, you test, discard, and set actions. Some choices may fit naturally the first time. Others may have to be rejected before you discover an interpretation that works. I come from the practical school of acting, where you test action. You do it, fix it, change it, adjust it, rather than thinking about action, analyzing it, researching it, and discussing it. Both schools are important, but because you must *play* a scene, the sooner you can get on your feet and test actions, the better.

Begin by establishing the physical framework of the sequence. Find out what your character is wearing. Then experiment with what task your character could be doing. If you choose a task like "to study," you might investigate your character's particular routine. What might your character do when studying? Would you paint your fingernails, sip hot tea, flick on the radio, sharpen pencils? Start by imagining items you could use on your desk. Possible objects might include cards, papers, food, prayer beads, cups, or liquor. Rehearse with different objects.

Keep those that provoke the most interesting thoughts and reactions.

What is a main action?

Besides a physical task, look for your character's main action, that is, the major thing you are doing in a scene. In any scene, usually one person is doing something and another is resisting it. Commit yourself to your main action, so you will buffer any opposition to it. Notice which major action works best with your lines. When possible, work closely with the other actors. The opposing actions you choose will set up the structure of the scene. In fact, the tension of a scene is caused by this collision of actions.

To get yourself into the action, experiment with playing it in the moments before a scene begins. Let's say, for example, that your character is a famous writer who has been hounded by critics. The play opens with the unexpected arrival of the critics. Your action upon entering is "to kick the critics out." You might imagine, offstage, that you have been battling for a week with *New York Times* reporters. When you recognize them, you play your action with venom. You hurl abuse.

Examples of main actions that propel characters in scenes are "to advance and to retreat," "to trap and to escape," "to confront and to ignore," "to collect and to hide the money," "to brag and to ignore," "to seduce and to withdraw." With strong main actions, the tension in a scene mounts. The lines gain weight and meaning. The phrase "I'm playing opposite so-and-so" really means that you are playing action *against* someone else's. Your main actions collide. (In monologues, you could be playing against another side of yourself.)

How do minor actions support my main action?

Besides choosing your main action, you must experiment with how you play the actions in different beats. If, for example, you are insulting the critics, you must listen for how they receive that action before proceeding to the next one. All action grows out of reaction. When you connect with a living, breathing actor, you will adapt your actions to affecting her. These minor actions or strategies keep you in the moment. Remember, variety provokes interest, so you're searching for contrast in your approach to different beats.

For example, if your main action is "to hurl abuse," test the smaller actions you are playing to get this across. Imagine yourself in similar circumstances. For instance, you might remember a time you tried to force someone out. What did you do? Yell, threaten, curse, toss things? How did the sequences change based on the responses you provoked?

In the following scene from *Death of a Salesman*, one actor tests the action "to retreat" for an opening beat. He has jotted down some possible line-by-line actions such as complaining, moaning, blaming, next to the text. Note: Write down your actions in pencil so you can adjust them as rehearsals proceed.

DEATH OF A SALESMAN: **NOTES ON WILLY'S OPENING BEAT**

Possible action: to retreat

ACTIONS

To moan	Linda:	(*hearing WILLY outside the bedroom, calls with some trepidation*) Willy!
	Willy:	It's all right. I came back.
	Linda:	Why? What happened? (*Slight pause.*) Did something happen, Willy?
To avoid	Willy:	No, nothing happened.
	Linda:	You didn't smash the car, did you?
To needle	Willy:	(*with casual irritation*) I said nothing happened. Didn't you hear me?
	Linda:	Don't you feel well?
To complain	Willy:	I'm tired to death. (*The flute has faded away. He sits on the bed beside her, a little numb.*) I couldn't make it. I just couldn't make it, Linda.

	Linda:	(*very carefully, delicately*) Where were you all day? You look terrible.
To collapse; to blame	Willy:	I got as far as a little above Yonkers. I stopped for a cup of coffee. Maybe it was the coffee.

But the breathtaking part of it all was not so much the planning as the fantastic skill with which the planning was concealed.

Eva Le Gallienne, *The Mystic in the Theatre: Eleonora Duse*

How should I rehearse actions line by line?

Line-by-line actions are the tiny doings you play on or between your different lines. Sometimes line-by-line actions oppose what you say. But normally what you are doing supports the words. For example, the action "to startle" might underlie the line "Gotcha!"

Find an action for each line and moment. In art, we judge greatness by the virtuosity of the sequence of actions—the way a ballerina spins a pirouette, a violinist builds to a high note. You, too, can develop an exciting moment-to-moment plan for a role. Remember, genius is 1 percent inspiration and 99 percent perspiration!

You can discover actions in various ways. Work out the approach that's best for you. Acting involves making choices. There is this group of actions that is going to say this, and this group of other actions that is going to say that. Which way is best? Try out different approaches and see. Look for choices that affect you emotionally.

Be as spontaneous as possible during the rehearsal process. In French, the word for "rehearsal," *essay*, means "an attempt."

During rehearsals, you try on actions for expressiveness. Gradually you piece small units into bigger and bigger sequences. Work as much as you can in detail, and keep in mind the overall action of the scene. You will be discovering ideas for small sections and intermittently reviewing larger sections of the play to build the sweep of the scenes and acts.

Find time to practice daily, unit by unit, so you can string together an interesting progression of actions. It is far better to rehearse twenty minutes daily than two hours once a week. Daily rehearsals develop your memory and imagination. Stopping rehearsal with partial work done stimulates you to do homework, ruminate, and return invigorated with fresh insights.

How should I rehearse the build of a scene?

As you grow comfortable with line-by-line actions and beats, focus rehearsals on discovering the momentum of the scene. In her autobiography, the actress Tallulah Bankhead gave this advice: "I'm the foe of moderation, the champion of excess. If I may lift a line from a die-hard whose identity is lost in the shuffle, I'd rather be strongly wrong than weakly right."

A compelling series of actions ripens your emotions. But keep a lid on them. Your actions must build to the climax of the scene. The audience feels more for you if you are trying to hold yourself together than if you're falling apart. Never play all you are experiencing.

Some artists defy others with their actions, especially during climactic scenes. One actress playing a grieving mother chose bold physical actions to communicate her grief. When her dead little girl's rag doll was tossed onto the floor, she broke free of those consoling her, dashed across the stage, and flung herself down on the doll. Another actress simulated possession by the devil. Audiences of young and old stood up and blocked others' view to see how the actress was hissing to attract the devil, writhing with pleasure, her tongue out, her eyes rolled back. Both actresses' extreme choices for action arose from insightful observation and rehearsal. They pushed the boundaries of self-expression with the range of truthful actions building inside their performances.

How do I prepare for a scene?

Besides preparing with physical warm-ups for the body, you must prepare for the scene's action emotionally. You do this by getting in touch with your character's action before your first entrance. Some actors come to the theater early and use the time while getting into costume and makeup to start thinking the thoughts (psychological actions) of the character before the entrance.

Others improvise the offstage life of the character and actually practice different improvisations during final rehearsals. At some point before your entrance you'll need to isolate yourself from backstage reality and focus on the character's offstage action. Allow yourself at least ten minutes. Often, choosing a physical action your character might do right before entering helps concentration. For example, if you're fixing yourself up for a date in your first stage action, you could start combing your hair offstage.

■ IMPROVISATION

What is improvisation?

Improvisation is the act of composing a sequence without previous study or preparation, spontaneously reacting to your fellow actors on stage in a relaxed and truthful way. Extemporizing develops impulses as a primary tool; you must rely on them.

How does improvisation help rehearsal?

Improvisation is a method for testing action in rehearsal. Until you set your interpretation for a scene, you are improvising to some extent. You are reacting with lines and movements in new ways to express your impulses. You are trying out choices to see which ones bring the strongest results from other characters. Experimenting with different approaches helps you discover nuances of meaning. You will find the appropriate impulses for a scene and the actions they lead to.

Improvisation can teach you about your character. In rehearsal, set up specific improvisations to help you relate truthfully as the character. Establish a given framework, then invent the scene spontaneously, using your own words. If you are playing a farewell scene, try saying goodbye in different ways. Or do the opposite: Improvise the time you first met.

Memory of the real encounter will thicken your relationship in the departure scene.

What are structured improvisations?

The progressive exercises at the end of each chapter of this book can be viewed as structured improvisations. They are structured in that they are rehearsed and have a framework supporting them. They are improvisations in that, though rehearsed, the verbal exchange is somewhat fluid. Progressive exercises excite your feelings by filtering more and more background into each encounter. Information leads to detail in your choices and to specific actions.

After you restage an improvisation, it becomes a "structured" improvisation because you have chosen elements to keep. Most acting in plays begins in a free format and develops a tighter and tighter structure Your challenge is to stay in touch with your impulses and the spontaneity originally felt in rehearsal. You are making the frozen format as exciting as the free. You are acting as if it's the first time.

■ CHECKLIST

1. Have you broken your scene down into beats?

2. What is your major action?

3. Have you physicalized your actions?

4. Do you have line-by-line actions?

■ FINAL PROJECTS

1. *Progressive Exercise.* Throughout the next several chapters, you will pursue a new series of related exercises. Each uses an element of chapters 1–5 to strengthen your

acting. Rehearse each sequence several times with your partner.

EXERCISE 1:   Pick a partner. You are strangers with opposing actions who meet at a spa or ski lodge.

Begin the scene in silence with each of you engaged in a physical activity. Then one of you should begin the verbal conflict where your main actions are in total opposition. Hand in your homework on the exercise, including your background notes and an outline of your main action.

2. *Sequencing Actions.* Choose a major action and a series of actions for one of the following descriptive sequences from a play. (One example has been partially completed.) Test various possibilities, then stage the most interesting one in class.

Buried Child by Sam Shepard, Act 1

ACTIONS:

OVERALL ACTION: <u>TO RELAX SELF</u>

1. to stare _____

2. to check _____

_____ distraction

3. to follow _____

_____ program

_____

_____

_____

_____

_____

_____

(*Gradually the form of* DODGE *is made out, sitting on the couch,* [1] *facing the TV. . . .* DODGE *slowly tilts his head back* [2] *and stares at the ceiling for a while, listening to the rain.* [3] *He lowers his head again and stares at the TV. He turns his head slowly to the left and stares at the sofa next to the one he's sitting on. He pulls his left arm out from under the blanket, slides his hand under the cushion, and pulls out a bottle of whiskey. He looks down left toward the staircase, listens, then uncaps the bottle, takes a long swig and caps it again. He puts the bottle back under the cushion and stares at the TV. He starts to cough slowly and softly. The coughing gradually builds. He holds one hand to his mouth and tries to stifle it. The coughing gets louder, then suddenly stops when he hears the sound of his wife's voice coming from the top of the staircase.*)

'Night, Mother by Marsha Norman

ACTIONS: **OVERALL ACTION:** _____

_____   *(MAMA stretches to reach the cupcakes in a cabinet*
                                in the kitchen. She can't see them, but she can feel
_____   *around for them, and she's eager to have one, so*
                                she's working pretty hard at it. This may be the
_____   *most serious exercise MAMA ever gets. She finds*
                                a cupcake, the coconut-covered, raspberry-and-
_____   *marshmallow-filled kind known as a snowball, but*
                                sees that there's one missing from the package.
_____   *She calls to JESSIE, who is apparently somewhere*
                                else in the house.)
_____

_____

Serenading Louie by Lanford Wilson (Hill & Wang, 1985), Act 1, Scene 1

ACTIONS: **OVERALL ACTION:** _____

_____   *(Nearly evening. The only light is on the desk)*
                                Carl: *(Coming from the kitchen as he closes the*
_____   *outside door, he calls from offstage)* Sweetheart?
                                (he enters) Honey? . . . Mary?
_____   *(he yells up the stairs)* Hey, baby? *(He goes to the*
                                patio door, yells out) Mary?
_____   *(He shuts the door, turns, and sees the light; he goes*
                                to the desk, picks up a note, and sits as he reads it.
_____   *He lets the note float from his hand back to the desk,*
                                shuts his eyes a moment, reaches to the desk lamp,
_____   *and turns it off.)* (Blackout)

_____

The Ghost Sonata by August Strindberg, Scene 1

ACTIONS: **OVERALL ACTION:** _____

_____   *(The milkmaid comes in from around the corner,*
                                carrying a wire basket filled with bottles. She is
_____   *wearing a summer dress, with brown shoes, black*
                                stockings and a white cap. She takes off her cap
_____   *and hangs it on the drinking fountain; wipes the*

_____ *sweat from her brow; takes a drink from the cup;*
washes her hands; arranges her hair, using the
_____ *water in the fountain as a mirror.*)

3. *Sibling Rivalry.* Stage a scene between two siblings, such as the greeting scene between Blanche and Stella in *A Streetcar Named Desire* or the bedroom scene between Biff and Happy in *Death of a Salesman.* Choose psychological and physical traits that reflect the character's and your own uniqueness. Make sure the actions of the two siblings totally clash.

4. *Framing the Action.* Do a physical task for two minutes while you focus on an action. Then let the task evolve into a monologue. Look for ways to physicalize your actions. The following monologue is partially analyzed to demonstrate the process. Additional monologues are in Appendix D.

Ludlow Fair by Lanford Wilson

ACTIONS: TASK: <u>TO SET MY HAIR</u>

1. to destroy _____   Agnes: [1][*Throw down old rollers*] [2]I'm going to be
                         a mess tomorrow. [3]I probably won't make it to work,
2. to complain _____   let alone lunch. [4]A casual lunch, [5][*Toss a bobby pin*
                         in trash] [6]my God. I wonder what he'd think—stupid
3. to predict _____   Charles—if he knew I was putting up my hair for
                         him; catching pneumonia. No lie, I can't wait till
4. to qualify _____   summer to see what kind of sunglasses he's going
                         to pop into the office with. Probably those World's
5. to mock _____   Fair charmers. A double unisphere. (*Turns*) Are
                         you going to sleep? (*Pause. No reply*) Well, crap.
6. to curse _____

_____

2
OBJECTIVE
What do I want?

This chapter deals with objective: what your character wants.

You will become as small as your controlling desire, as great as your dominant aspiration.

James Allen

■ WHAT IS AN OBJECTIVE?

An objective is what your character wants. It's the character's reason for doing something. In each beat or bit of stage life, just as in real life, you're doing something (action) because you're wanting something (objective). In life, your desires are so close to you they are often unconscious; onstage, you must get in touch with the longings, conscious and unconscious, of your character. The more these consume your thoughts, the more psychological actions will pop into your head.

Also called an intention, purpose, or need, an objective motivates your action. For instance, the objectives "to enrapture you," "to torment you," "to seduce you," and "to amuse you" would stimulate different actions. Basically, your actions—the way you move, talk, get a drink, and so forth—are directed toward reaching your objective—what you want from someone.

Be sure that what you do is shaped by what you want. For example, onstage you don't just eat your dinner. You do so in a way that tells another character something about what you want—for example, a date, some money. You choose a way to eat your dinner that is more instructive than another, equally possible way.

Do objectives change?

Your objective may change onstage. After getting what you want (for example, you get the date), you might then shift to a different one. Similarly, if you fail to get what you want (for example, you get rejected), you might try another objective. Continue to pursue your objective until you succeed or another objective replaces it. For example, if your objective is "to get a free room at a motel," and the manager responds negatively to the action "to flatter," another appropriate action—for example, "to humor"—might be necessary to fulfill the desire. In fact, a more interesting scene usually develops if you choose not to like what you get.

You are agitated by the other character's manner of presentation. You feel the other character could have been sweeter, smarter, more considerate in the going. Or you immediately want something else. Your obsessions penetrate below the dialogue and fire you to achieve satisfaction.

You are trying to get through to someone, to change her, to make him feel a certain way. In moving that person, you move the audience. Note in the "Bus Observation" that follows how objectives motivate action.

BUS OBSERVATION

Scene: a bus in New Orleans

Objective: to win sympathy from the driver

ACTION	OBJECTIVE
1. to hurry onto the bus	1. to win approval from the driver
2. to slug change into the fare box	2. to win approval from the driver
3. to look for twenty more cents	3. to win approval from the driver
4. to scramble inside my bag	4. to stall the driver

5. to dump out my wallet

6. to moan

7. to rub my back

8. to check my pockets

9. to wave my eviction notice

10. to droop my shoulders

11. to ransack my bag for change

12. to slam more change into box

13. to knife the driver with a dirty look

14. to stride down the aisle

5. to stall

6. to soften the driver

7. to soften

8. to soften

9. to overcome the driver

10. to overcome

11. to overcome

12. to punish the driver

13. to punish

14. to pulverize the driver

How do I name objectives?

To name objectives in a scene, ask yourself, "What do I want now, and from whom?" You can do an improvisation to help you name objectives. In the following example, an actress has jotted down objectives she discovered when improvising a series of actions for a scene. Note that I call this a structured exercise because it has a hidden plan supporting it.

STRUCTURED EXERCISE: BLANCHE'S ENTRANCE

A Streetcar Named Desire by Tennessee Williams, Scene 1

Observe how the actor changes objectives by breaking her sequence into a beginning, middle, and end.

OBJECTIVE	ACTIONS
	Beginning
to alert any vagrants inside	to enter
	to close the door
	to listen for sounds
	to drop the suitcase
	to scan the living/dining room
	to look for messages

OBJECTIVE	ACTIONS
	Middle
to reassure myself I am welcome here	to explore the apartment
	to scan the papers on the table
	to tiptoe into the bedroom
	to reexplore the living room
	to worry when Stella will be back
	End
to overcome my shock	to find some liquor
	to scan the living room
	to rummage through a cabinet
	to search in the drawers
	to peer under a couch
	to slip into the kitchen
	to spot liquor
	to hurry into the living room
	to perch on the couch
	to gulp the liquor
	to relax
	to lean back on the couch
	to calm self

Why should I use active verbs?

When naming objectives, use the infinitive form of an active verb. An active objective is easier to play. For example, "to excite Stella" is more dynamic than "wanting to make Stella enthusiastic about my coming to her house." Try to word your objective so that it inspires you to pursue the action. For example, some objectives might be:

> to con money from Oscar
>
> to arouse Ophelia
>
> to annihilate Macduff
>
> to slug Maggie

Try violent, provocative, or even sexual verbs. No one but you knows the words you're using, so make your objectives ones that excite you!

EXERCISES

1. *My Secret.* Talk truthfully about yourself. Who are you? Where do you come from? What do you hope to gain from the class (objective)? Then share one secret desire.

2. *My Dream.* What is the biggest desire you have right now? To get into a great school? To marry someone? To save your parents' marriage? To become a famous actor? Share this dream with the class. Identify someone in a play or film who is playing the same objective. Optional: Stage a scene from this play or film.

What are strong objectives?

Lord, grant that I may always desire more than I can accomplish.

Michelangelo

Strong objectives focus your attention and compel you to risk daring action. Observe which of your needs arouses a physical sensation, making you breathe heavily, break out in a cold sweat, clear your throat. Imagine the source of that need in various parts of your body (your heart, your throat, your groin). For example, "wanting to impress a severe biology teacher" dries up my mouth. Strong objectives often excite a physical response. Note how the following objectives differ in forcefulness:

WEAK OBJECTIVE	POWERFUL OBJECTIVE
1. to have you hear this story	1. to mesmerize you
2. to transcend your superiority	2. to crush you
3. to give you some comical information	3. to convulse you with laughter
4. to get your attention	4. to galvanize you

A well-written scene may work even when you play thin objectives, but fiery ones will make it even more astonishing. Always try playing a stronger need than initially occurs to you.

Objectives, like wishes, are often secrets. Some of the forcefulness of your objective may come from the fact that it is hidden. Objectives gnaw away at you. They delude you into believing that if only they would materialize, satisfaction would ensue. Although you anticipate winning, whatever you are craving moment to moment you usually don't get.

How do objectives counteract anticipation?

Strong objectives impel you to change another character's outlook and thus overcome anticipation. Each character pursues an objective that is often the opposite of what happens. If you expect what happens, you will begin jumping ahead of yourself in the scene. Onstage, you are usually adjusting moves based on new information. For example, if your character anticipates a marriage proposal, expecting what she doesn't get (a proposal) makes rejection the more painful. You might play the objective "to win approval." You might keep imagining moment to moment his slipping that ring onto your finger. Wanting that ring will hurl you into deeper conflict.

In some instances, a character's intelligence might assure correct anticipation of what is to come, but he might misjudge how he will feel when specific needs are thwarted. Where possible, drift in the direction of false hope for a strong objective so as to startle yourself when different information is delivered.

■ OPPOSING OBJECTIVES

How do you find strong major objectives?

A major objective is your overall need in a scene. The effectiveness of your major objective results from opposition. Warring objectives create electricity onstage. When you need something that is blocked by something or someone, the suspense mounts.

Analyzing the closing of the scene to determine what your character has or hasn't obtained will often reveal your major objective. Or you may have to discover one that works for you. If your character enters to talk to someone who is sitting anxiously on a couch, your major objective is "to relax her." But not every actor doing that scene has to work from that objective. You can find another one, such as "to cheer her," that works for you.

Strong objectives require opposition. In most scenes, the objectives of the major characters collide. For example, one character wants "to excite," and the other wants "to quiet" the other. One character wishes "to bewitch," and the other wishes "to distance" the other. When alone, a character may play opposites within herself.

When you are onstage with someone else, even when it is not apparent in the dialogue, that other character's objective differs from yours. Warring objectives even ground the love scene. In *Romeo and Juliet*, Romeo wants to seduce Juliet, and Juliet, fearing for Romeo's life, wants him to leave.

How can another person block my objective?

Onstage, you are continually trying to get your desire fulfilled through someone: another person, the audience, a wiser self, or a remembered person. The most frequent confrontation occurs between two passionate people. One person's desire provokes another. Observe the opposing objectives in the following segment from act 1, scene 2 of Eugene O'Neill's *Beyond the Horizon*. Andrew wants to break free from his family. His father, mother, and brother are obsessed with keeping him home on the farm. Opposing objectives often represent two sides of the same coin.

Andrew: (*facing his father*) I agree with you, Pa, and I tell you again, once and for all, that I've made up my mind to go [and leave the farm].

Mayo: (*dumbfounded—unable to doubt the determination in Andrew's voice—helplessly*) But why, Son? Why?

Andrew:	(*evasively*) I've always wanted to go.
Robert:	Andy!
Andrew:	(*half angrily*) You shut up, Rob! (*Turning to his father again*) I didn't ever mention it because as long as Rob was going I knew it was no use; but now Rob's staying on here, there isn't any reason for me not to go.
Mayo:	(*breathing hard*) No reason? Can you stand there and say that to me, Andrew?
Mrs. Mayo:	(*hastily—seeing the gathering storm*) He doesn't mean a word of it, James.
Mayo:	(*making a gesture to her to keep silence*) Let me talk, Katey. (*In a more kindly tone*) What's come over you so sudden, Andy? You know's well as I do that it wouldn't be fair o' you to run off at a moment's notice right now when we're up to our necks in hard work.
Andrew:	(*avoiding his eyes*) Rob'll hold his end up as soon as he learns.
Mayo:	Robert was never cut out for a farmer, and you was.
Andrew:	You can easily get a man to do my work.
Mayo:	(*restraining his anger with an effort*) It sounds strange to hear you, Andy, that I always thought had good sense, talkin' crazy like that. (*Scornfully*) Get a man to take your place! You ain't been workin' here for no hire, Andy, that you kin give me your notice to quit like you've done.

At their peak, such clashing objectives strip you and your opponent bare. Note Robert's and Ruth's speeches later, in act 2, scene 1, where husband and wife who have stayed on the farm play the objective "to destroy each other."

| Ruth: | What do you think—living with a man like you—having to suffer all the time because you've never been man enough to work and do things like other people. But no! You never own up to that. You think you're so much better than other folks, with your college education, where you never learned a thing, and always reading your stupid books instead of working. I s'pose you think I ought to |

be *proud to* be your wife—a poor, ignorant thing like me! (*Fiercely*) But I'm not. I hate it! I hate the sight of you. Oh, if I'd only known! If I hadn't been such a fool to listen to your cheap, silly, poetry talk that you learned out of books! If I could have seen how you were in your true self—like you are now—I'd have killed myself before I'd have married you! I was sorry for it before we'd been together a month. I knew what you were really like—when it was too late.

Robert: (*his voice raised loudly*) And now—I'm finding out what you're really like—what a—a creature I've been living with. (*With a harsh laugh*) God! It wasn't that I haven't guessed how mean and small you are—but I've kept on telling myself that I must be wrong—like a fool!—like a damned fool!

Imagine you are Ruth or Robert. What urgent needs could spark this dialogue? Imagine what's going on inside you. How are you breathing? How do your eyes feel? Is your throat dry? What are you putting on the line in this confrontation?

How can the audience assist with my objective?

Some characters' most intimate encounters occur when confronting the audience in a monologue. You must figure out why your character can't reveal herself to the other characters but bares her soul to the audience instead. It varies play to play, and character to character. What do you want from the audience?

Troubled characters often reach out to the audience to solve a burning problem. A character contemplating suicide could urge the audience (as a wiser presence) to tell him what to do. Imagine Hamlet playing the following lines as needing the answer from the audience:

Hamlet: To be, or not to be, that is the question:
Whether 'tis nobler in the mind to suffer
The slings and arrows of outrageous fortune,
Or to take arms against a sea of troubles
And by opposing end them. To die, to sleep—
No more; and by a sleep to say we end

The heart-ache and the thousand natural shocks
That flesh is heir to: 'tis a consummation
Devoutly to be wish'd.

How do you confront yourself?

Besides addressing the audience, you often talk to—even battle with—yourself. Imagine the conversation you had with yourself when you were contemplating telling a lie to get a job, for example. You were in a dilemma, and you expected a wiser part of yourself to respond. You were asking yourself something and logically anticipating a solution. In times of stress you might summon a wiser self for advice. You could talk to yourself to keep from cracking up, to gain control over your circumstances, to test your sanity, to keep yourself in reality, to calm yourself. The simple fact that you talk to yourself means one part of you seeks to control another. Even when alone, find two sides of the self that are warring. One side wants something it isn't getting from another side.

How can I confront someone offstage?

When alone onstage, you may want something from someone who has departed or who is arriving. You may test out what you just said or what you plan to say. When somebody exits, your character may continue confronting him, or you may begin daydreaming about your next interaction. You may be dissatisfied, or so satisfied that you want more from the next encounter.

Your actions are motivated even by the memory of a person. For example, you might want to tear open the windows because your heartthrob is coming. Maybe you nuzzle a shirt in hopes of picking up a lover's scent. Perhaps you smash your heel into the glass of a photograph. When the audience senses your needs via characters who are offstage or only talked about, you are becoming convincingly real.

■ OBJECTIVES IN EACH RELATIONSHIP

Now that you understand objectives, let's look at how relationships affect them. A relationship is an invisible link between characters. This link stimulates specific desires. Your character's way of talking, touching, listening may differ drastically depending on whether you want something from your greedy mother, your spoiled self, an offstage idol, or hostile patrons. If you want to get the car keys from your father versus from an offstage robber, your actions vary. You might "charm your father," "flatter him," "do him a favor," "show him a good grade"; whereas you might "scream," "beg on your knees," or "bribe the robber."

Relationships give rise to specific objectives. I want my sister to support me because she is my sister, and I expect support from my family. I want to protect my lover, and I expect him to act responsibly. I want to embrace my bride because I love her. You crave specific things from prying relatives, scolding friends, and jeering enemies.

How are my relationships personalized?

Your character's relationship should touch you personally. Personalize what the other character means to you. Does the other character have a temper like your mother's, scolding eyes like your dad's, a sense of humor like your best friend's? Perhaps what you want from your stage sister more closely resembles something you want from your real-life cousin.

Begin by relating what you want from the other character to an entanglement in your own life. Ask yourself, "If she was actually my sister, wife, or best friend, what would I want? How would I behave?" If the analogy doesn't work, choose any real person who resembles the other character. Associate the two, such as by relating that both are dark-eyed, German, possessive, or stubborn. Then play the scene to that real person within the body of the actor playing the character.

You can personalize relationships onstage by how you do the action. Imagine now the intricate ways you interact with your own father. The audience won't accept an actor as your father unless you treat him like a real father. Ask yourself, "What do I do when I want to cheer my father up? Whistle a tune? Wrestle? Slap palms? Grab his shoulders?" If appropriate, try doing these actions and see whether they stimulate the necessary thoughts, feelings, sensations to personalize the relationship.

For a farewell scene, fantasize a departure you had with someone close to you. After the personalization is wedded in your heart, drop this adjustment. You will experience needing something from that other character. Make sure the relationship has a strong hook into you, much like a hook in a fish's mouth. Not only do you respond to these tugs, but also each tug wounds you.

How do physical relationships drive my objectives?

The day is gone, and all its sweets are gone! Sweet voice, sweet lips, soft hand, and softer breast. O for a life of Sensations rather than of Thoughts!

John Keats, letter to Benjamin Bailey, November 22, 1817

Your emotions make themselves known through physical sensations. Cliché phrases like "This person tickles my fancy," "makes my stomach churn," "sets my heart racing," or "leaves me cold" indicate sensual responses. Ask yourself, "How does the other character affect me physically?"

Notice what you do when you're excited by a suitor, when you're hungry for a hug from Mother, when you're thwarted by a superior. How does your body adjust? What thoughts and sensations are provoked by this bodily reaction? What do you do?

How do psychological relationships stimulate my desires?

Do you allude to me, Miss Cardew, as an entanglement?

Gwendolen, *The Importance of Being Earnest* by Oscar Wilde, act 2

Onstage, observe how a psychological relationship drives your desires. Putting certain mental conditions on a relationship can sharpen your impulses. For example, two characters are onstage. The boy is reading the newspaper. The girl is sipping coffee. Let's specify the psychological condition "in love." If they've been dating for six months and are getting married, they may crave closeness. They may share the coffee cup. He may hold her hand. They may read the paper together. This could excite her. Conversely, if the couple has been dating for six years, they may be a bit blasé; they might need some space. They could take each other for granted. He might devour the paper. Annoyed, she might motion to him to pass the toast as she sips nonchalantly. Their needs result from different mental relationships dictating responsiveness onstage.

Why is responsiveness important?

Responsiveness, or the electricity between characters, is what is present when actors refer to a scene as "cooking."

You can sometimes evoke the fullest responsiveness by rekindling the sensations of your dreams. Dreams awaken you to the ambiguity of your needs. To expand responsiveness, suppose: "If this were a nightmare (fantasy), what desire would my character want met by this relationship?" Imagine yourself, as in a dream, to be overtaken by the encounter. Open yourself to the unpredictable. Try to relinquish your inhibitions so that you can travel with the relationship in the powerful direction that it is running. Begin experiencing the fantastic needs of each relationship.

EXERCISES

1. *Farewell.* Improvise a farewell situation. Stage the sequence first realistically, then in an exaggerated way, as if in a nightmare.

2. *Emergency Room.* Do an improvisation in which one of you plays an admitting clerk at a hospital emergency room and

another a patient seeking help. Choose a physical relation-ship (strong bodily response) based on the fact that the patient is one of the following: a prostitute, long-lost friend, foreigner, doctor, your mother, your brother, a rival in love, your therapist.

3. *Crawling Babies.* Blindfolded, imagine yourselves as crawl-ing babies. Explore another actor through touch. Describe his her physical characteristics. Then identify the names of neighbors you bump into.

4. *Touch Me.* Heighten physical chemistry with another by cre-ating five instances when you touch in a different place in a scene.

■ REHEARSING OBJECTIVES

What should I focus on in rehearsals?

React to specific words and actions, as coming from specific people, from whom you want specific things. Respond to what that actor is giving you in the present. Is he fulfilling your ob-jective right now? When you go onstage, the question is, "Am I persuading you to give me what I want?" Onstage, you should be asking, "Are you understanding me?" You must experi-ence another character *right now*, relating to—and usually resisting—you. Keep your objective with another actor alive, as something you must fulfill *now*. Focus on the present.

Onstage, your character is tied to the other character, like a water skier to a speedboat. Fantasize how dramatically you respond when it races ahead, turns, stalls, stops. You are re-sponding continually; reactions occur not only on the line, but also before you say a line, after you speak, in all your reactions. Play a scene as if the character opposite you is the most aston-ishing creature you've ever met.

Concentrate on that actor so fully you don't have time to think about yourself.

Repetitious exercises help to tie your objectives to the other character. Needing to repeat the other's gesture exactly encourages you to keep focused on him. If you are looking for some slight change in another's behavior, you have to listen with your whole being to see whether she's meeting that objective. Being sensitive to what that individual is doing, you respond truthfully to her every move.

EXERCISES

1. *Repetitious Exercise.* Repeat what you hear your partner saying five or six times, then ask for something. Continue this pattern for several minutes, back and forth. Focus on staying with your partner's every move. Decide on a relationship. Stage a sequence of repetitions to reveal it. Some subjects that the partner could talk about include your outlook, your looks, your health. For example: "You're looking very ill," "I'm looking very ill," repeated six or seven times. Then: "You're feeling better," "I'm feeling better," and so forth.

2. *Silent Task.* Pair off. Decide on a relationship, be it conventional, such as parent-child or sister-brother, or unconventional. Use some specific activity, such as making a salad, packing a suitcase, straightening the room, during which you must respond to each other without using words to communicate what the relationship is.

3. *Improvising Relationships.* List ten qualities that suggest a couple who has been married five years, as opposed to ten or fifteen years. Stage an improvisation in silence, implementing these ten qualities. Be sure to include a physical task; for example, the way you set the table may telegraph a comfortable marriage.

4. *A Complete Relationship.* Stage a brief scene from a play. Focus rehearsals on developing a complete relationship.

Then rehearse the scene with a different interpretation of the same relationship as it is two years later. Stage both versions in class.

Should I get to know other actors?

The more comfortable you are with other actors, the better you can play your objectives. Trust encourages you to react intuitively as the character. Use rehearsal to get to know other actors, so you can manipulate, bargain with, hypnotize, bewitch them onstage to get what you want.

Sometimes you may have to show affection toward an actor whom you dislike. Find a way to neutralize your negativity. For example, if she is playing your wife, imagine that she inherited an annoying trait from her mother, whom you don't like anyway. So you dislike her mother's fault, but your wife is perfect.

If possible, spend time offstage with anybody your character relates to onstage. If not, observe his picture, find out about him, watch his behavior offstage. You want an opinion about that actor, a physical response to him. Try to discover what you admire or resent about him. It may be something unspoken, but if you notice that the actor playing your boss has a nervous habit of chewing on the edge of his nail, it could strengthen your resistance if it makes you cringe. Offstage, an actor you dine with may continually freshen her makeup. You could use this information onstage, in a scene where you compliment the character, a rival, on her looks.

How do I work off another actor?

To work off another actor, you must experience what you want that is residing in her. You need to do something to her to get what you want. In rehearsals, practice stirring up the actor playing opposite you so that she is in a different state by the end of the scene. For example, make her concerned rather than complacent, enthusiastic rather than bored, compassionate rather than angry. Remember, when you move that other person, you move the audience.

You transform a concept such as "to seduce" into a real experience by relating to the other actor. What do you like about him? How does he make you feel? What about him (the texture of his hair, warmth of his fingers, his radiant humor) do you find irresistible? Find something compelling about the other actor. Allow yourself to be drawn to this quality. The intoxication of acting in a love scene opposite a great actor is that he convinces you that he is madly in love with you—so much so that you must resist pursuing his affections offstage.

What should I look for in the other actor onstage?

To keep your objective alive, observe what the other actor is doing. See whether you are getting your need met. Initially you may need to practice the scene slowly, to let the other actor "move in on you"—a professional term meaning to experience you onstage. Mark places in your script where you check to see whether you're getting what you want. Is the other actor as happy or sad as you wanted? Measure whether you are succeeding in meeting your objective by the reactions you provoke.

What should I listen for?

Listen to determine whether you're getting your objective. In real life, we can sometimes allow our minds to wander. But actors must listen. Listen with specific focus on what you want from a relationship. Interpret the meaning of each message to the relationship. For instance, you are uncovering your groom's motivations, your brother's disdain. When listening closely, you are intent on experiencing the thoughts, feelings, sensations of another. Try to perceive what the other actor is giving you in this relationship. Sensitize yourself to nuances of his behavior. You are listening for his objective so that you can immediately respond in character.

■ CHECKLIST

1. Am I playing strong objectives?
2. Who or what is blocking them?
3. Are my relationships personalized?
4. Am I listening to get my objective?

■ FINAL PROJECTS

1. *Progressive Exercise.* This exercise is related to the one in chapter 1, so you have the same partner. Rehearse this sequence several times.

   EXERCISE 2: A desolate cliff. Two years have passed since Progressive Exercise 1. You and your partner are intensely related. You each play a strong action with an objective.
   Many minor objectives and actions may also influence you in the scene.
   Begin the scene in silence with each of you engaged in a physical activity. Then one of you should begin the verbal conflict. Hand in your written backgrounds.

2. *Total Conflict.* Create a sequence with a partner in which a conflict erupts because you have totally different objectives. For example, your roommate wants to marry you and you decide to move overseas. Spend time discussing your relationship and setting up a specific place. Use the environment and the facts you make up to pursue your objective. Use real props to help you believe in the space and pick opposing objectives that truly provoke you. Start the improvisation with two minutes of silence in which you each do an activity that leads to the conflict. Then one of you should begin the verbal conflict.

3. *Open Scene.* Choose a specific relationship and place for the following scene. Make sure your and your partner's objec-

tives conflict. Each of you should pick one overall objective
to play, for example, "to make Adrian laugh," or "to wound
Pat." Do the first two minutes of the scene in silence. Each of
you should perform a physical task that leads to the conflict.
Focus on winning your objective. (Note that the scene is
called an open scene because it allows for a great range of
interpretation. Have fun!)

Adrian:	I'm just not ready.
Pat:	You don't want me to move in?
Adrian:	It's not that.
Pat:	You do want me to move in?
Adrian:	I don't know.
Pat:	Look, Adrian, this is ridiculous.
Adrian:	I know it's ridiculous.
Pat:	Then for God's sake make a decision. That's all I want.
Adrian:	I'm too tired.
Pat:	Adrian.
Adrian:	Can you wait one more day?
Pat:	No.
Adrian:	Well, I can't make the decision right now.
Pat:	Every time it ends this way.
Adrian:	Tomorrow, I promise. Really, really.
Pat:	I can't force you to make a decision. I'm warning you, though, it's getting to the point where I don't care.
Adrian:	(*pausing*) Eight o'clock?
Pat:	I guess.
Adrian:	I love you.
Pat:	Tomorrow.

4. *Monologue to an Individual.* Study the following monologue
that the poetic young Eugene addresses to Laura, his mother's beautiful new boarder, in act 1, scene 2 of Ketti Fring's
dramatization of Thomas Wolfe's novel *Look Homeward,*

Angel and identify a possible overall objective. Ask yourself what specifically you want the other person to experience. What major objective will you use to change that individual's emotional state? Find your major objective by practicing the monologue with another actor from class. Use active infinitives. Other possible monologue selections are cited in Appendix D.

OVERALL OBJECTIVE: "TO + VERB"

Eugene: Have you ever touched one? [. . .] A locomotive. [. . .] Have you ever put your hand on one? You have to feel things to fully understand them. Even a cold one, standing in a station yard. You know what you feel? You feel the shining steel rails under it— and the rails send a message right into your hand—a message of all the mountains that engine ever passed—all the flowing rivers, the forests, the towns, all the houses, the people, the washlines flapping in the fresh cool breeze—the beauty of the people in the way they live and the way they work—a farmer waving from his field, a kid from the school yard—the faraway places it roars through at night, places you don't even know, can hardly imagine. Do you believe it? You feel the rhythm of a whole life, a whole country clicking through your hand.

5. *Monologue to the Audience.* In small groups, practice the following monologue addressed to the audience from act 2 of *A View from the Bridge* by Arthur Miller. Focus on your objective, on what you want the other group members to feel. Identify the objective needed to move individuals from one frame of mind to the next. Make notes next to the text. Note: A forceful objective should change the audience's state of being.

OBJECTIVE (WHAT DO I WANT MY PARTNER [THE AUDIENCE] TO FEEL?):

Alfieri: On December twenty-seventh I saw him next. I normally go home well before six, but that day I sat around looking out my window at the bay, and when I saw him walking through my doorway, I knew why I had waited. And if I seem to tell this like a dream, it was that way. Several moments arrived in the course of the two talks we had when it occurred to me how—almost transfixed I had come to feel. I had lost my strength somewhere. (EDDIE *enters, removing his cap, sits in the chair, looks thoughtfully out*) I looked in his eyes more than I listened—in fact, I can hardly remember the conversation. But I will never forget how dark the room became when he looked at me; his eyes were like tunnels. I kept wanting to call the police, but nothing had happened. Nothing at all had really happened.

3
OBSTACLES
What's in my way?

This chapter deals with the elements that impede the action and thus create suspense. Your obstacle intensifies action by thwarting it.

We will either find a way or make one.

Hannibal

■ WHAT IS AN OBSTACLE?

An obstacle is something that stands in the way of your action. In every beat, you are doing something, wanting something, and something is stopping you. By blocking what you're pursuing, the obstacle creates unpredictability, which excites the audience to participate mentally. Think about how alert football players are when the score is tied with two minutes to go. The obstacle of a deadline is one that occurs frequently in both comedy and drama.

Why are obstacles important?

Actions require obstacles to sustain attention. Obstacles challenge you to intensify what you do. You have to pursue a full range of actions to overcome obstacles.

Note in the "Bus Observation" that follows how obstacles intensify action.

BUS OBSERVATION

Scene: A bus in New Orleans

Main Obstacle: Driver's indifference

ACTION	OBJECTIVE	OBSTACLES
1. to hurry onto the bus	to win approval from the driver	slippery floor
2. to slug change into the fare box	to win approval	thin coin slot
3. to look for twenty more cents	to win approval	empty wallet
4. to scramble inside my bag	to stall the driver	messy papers in bag
5. to dump out my wallet	to stall	too many photos in wallet
6. to moan	to soften the driver	no time
7. to rub my back	to soften	heavy topcoat
8. to check my pockets	to soften	pockets full of objects
9. to wave my eviction notice	to overcome the driver	other passengers' impatience
10. to droop my shoulders	to overcome	driver's indifference
11. to ransack my bag for change	to overcome	messy bag
12. to slam more change into the box	to punish the driver	broken fare box
13. to knife the driver with a dirty look	to punish	driver's indifference
14. to stride down the aisle	to pulverize the driver	unsteadiness on feet

Obstacles create the suspense in a scene. A carefully rehearsed plan of action, focused on overcoming the opposition, encourages the gradual growth of emotion and lends depth to your acting. To quote Stanislavski (*My Life in Art*): "What was good was that we saw how you controlled yourself more and more, until at last something tore into you, and you could control yourself no longer." Never play the obstacle—that is, don't telegraph how much it bothers you. Instead, focus on the action. You sustain audience interest by showing how much you can bear.

What is a major obstacle?

In every scene, your character struggles against a major obstacle, which blocks your main action. The other character usually creates this obstacle. Your opposing needs lead you to actions that clash in some way. To find the obstacle, ask, "What person is stopping me in each scene?"

The major obstacle to one character's persecuting his mother is her comforting him. An actor playing Hamlet once made the choice of the extreme action of throwing a corpse into his mother's lap and pushing the corpse's face into hers. This assault would block his mother's action of calming him down.

Major obstacles need not be negative. Young lovers might differ about whether to consummate their affection. Because of the suspense, the audience wants to know what will ensue.

Notice how the opposing objectives "to protect" and "to seduce" create the colliding actions of the young lovers in this excerpt from act 2, scene 2 of *Romeo and Juliet.*

Juliet: How came you hither, tell me, and wherefore?
          The orchard walls are high and hard to climb,
          And the place death, considering who you are,
          If any of my kinsmen find you here.

Romeo: With love's light wings did I o'erperch these walls;
          For stony limits cannot hold love out,
          And what love can do, that dares love attempt;
          Therefore your kinsmen are no stop to me.

Juliet: If they do see you they will murder you.

When actions clash, one of two outcomes can result: The actions of both of you are evenly blocked, or one of you overcomes the other.

EXERCISES

1. *Opposing Action.* List actions that oppose the following ones:

Objective: To abandon you
ACTION

Opposing Objective: To pick you up
OPPOSING ACTION

1. to pack my suitcase
2. to distance you
3. to change clothes
4. to leave
5. to write a paper
6. to practice my exercises
7. to straighten the room
8. to pay remaining bills

1. _____
2. _____
3. _____
4. _____
5. _____
6. _____
7. _____
8. _____

Consider the following opposing actions. How do they differ from the ones you wrote?

ACTION

1. to pack my suitcase
2. to distance you
3. to change clothes
4. to leave
5. to write a paper
6. to practice my exercises
7. to straighten the room
8. to pay remaining bills

OPPOSING ACTION

1. to unpack your suitcase
2. to embrace
3. to undress you
4. to corner you
5. to party
6. to dance with you
7. to ransack the room
8. to massage your feet

2. *Overcoming My Distance.* In pairs, practice throwing a ball back and forth. Keep widening the distance between you.

3. *Getting Attention.* Rehearse a sequence in which you play the objective "to seize another's attention" while he focuses on ignoring you. This can represent a major obstacle.

4. *Touching and Tension.* Rehearse a sequence using two or three different distance ranges between the characters. Study

the power of touch versus distance onstage in establishing the necessary tension in a scene.

What are minor obstacles?

Minor obstacles are smaller ones that fortify the major obstacle. They create variety by erupting unpredictably throughout a scene. In the following scene, which opens act 3 of Arthur Miller's *All My Sons*, Jim's major obstacle is Mother's silence about her missing son, Chris.

One actor playing Jim discovered minor obstacles by observing the conditions and thoughts that made playing the action more difficult. He noted his major need in a scene (to calm Mother) and the minor obstacles that blocked him (poor visibility, lateness, tiredness). Minor obstacles can extend for a period of time (like Mother's ceaseless rocking) or for just a few moments (like someone at the bedroom window).

ALL MY SONS: JIM'S OBSTACLES

Major Obstacle:
Mother's silence

Action: To make conversation

Possible Minor Obstacles:

Objective: To calm Mother

lateness

tiredness

rocking unnerves me

spooky moon

my previous search for him

Two o'clock the *following morning.* MOTHER *is discovered on the rise, rocking ceaselessly in a chair, staring at her thoughts. It is an intense, slight sort of rocking. A light shows from the upstairs bedroom, lower floor windows being dark. The moon is strong and casts its bluish light. Presently,* JIM, *dressed in jacket and hat, appears from the Left, and seeing her, goes up beside her.*

poor visibility

someone watching at bedroom window, when she doesn't sleep she cracks up

Jim: Any news?

Mother: No news.

Jim: (*gently*) You can't sit up all night, dear, why don't you go to bed?

ceaseless rocking	Mother:	I'm waiting for Chris. Don't worry about me, Jim, I'm perfectly all right.
seven hours of waiting	Jim:	But it's almost two o'clock.
	Mother:	I can't sleep. (*Slight pause*) You had an emergency?
her incessant prying the Muhlers	Jim:	(*tiredly*) Somebody had a headache and thought he was dying. (*Slight pause*) Half of my patients are quite mad. Nobody realizes how many people are walking around loose, and they're cracked as coconuts.
my new Ford her withdrawal she belittles me		Money. Money-money-money-money. You say it long enough. It doesn't mean anything. (*She smiles, makes a silent laugh*) Oh, how I'd love to be around when that happens.
her irritability	Mother:	(*shakes her head*) You're so child-ish, Jim. Sometimes you are.

Many minor obstacles strengthen action in this interpretation.

■ DISCOVERING OBSTACLES

What are physical obstacles?

Physical obstacles are natural barriers that block action externally. A blaring alarm that scares a thief when looting a building is a physical obstacle; so is a person like a tall guard who blocks a player when throwing a ball. Just as you look for physical actions to play, you should find physical obstacles. A physical obstacle communicates immediately with the audience and provides a tangible force that you can work against in a scene. Wherever possible, you should layer your work with physical obstacles because they are the easiest to control. It's much simpler to work against a tangible force than against a thought.

Physical obstacles trigger emotions because you don't have to *imagine* the obstacles. You simply play your action "to throw the ball," and a physical obstacle such as an opponent, distance, or a faulty glove creates the problem. A physical obstacle immediately agitates you. For example, if your action is "to get dressed," the obstacle of too-tight pants will frustrate you more than just thinking about being thin. Notice which items around you could stifle your action "to read" right now. Endless physical obstacles exist.

How can the place work as an obstacle?

The place can threaten your character's action. Think of how you've felt when walking to your car in a deserted parking lot or trying to sleep in a freezing apartment. Many locales automatically deter action. Some playwrights construct the environment as a major obstacle. Romeo wants to be in Juliet's bedroom rather than below the balcony. In another play, a character longs to roam outdoors rather than hide in the attic. In yet another, a character struggles to escape the ghetto.

A particular occasion in a particular place can inhibit action even further. Think of how you might act in church at the marriage of your fiancé to someone else, in the labor room at the birth of triplets, in the graveyard at the burial of your father. Whatever you choose to do on these occasions often has consequences. After a choice is made, you can't turn back. Key events—marriages, births, deaths, departures—in special places pressure the action of many characters: the auction of an estate, a secret forgery in a conventional community, a birthday at a Mississippi mansion, a hanging in Salem, an only brother's wedding in a small southern town, the purchase of a first house in postwar Chicago, the death of a child in Texas.

How can the place create real problems?

The place can create real problems by physically hindering you. We move more onstage than in real life. A floor plan that creates obstacles for the characters heightens interest in the action.

Allow physical conditions of your environment (such as noise, dirt, light) to agitate you. For example, if noise is stopping you from studying, you might move across the room, retreat under the covers, pound on the wall, or stuff cotton into your ears. When you are setting up the space, consider not putting everything within arm's reach. Cross to get your makeup or shaving kit as opposed to having it right next to you. Let the chair at a table be pushed in, so you must pull it out to sit down, just as you would in real life. If you are playing a love scene, start out across the room from your partner, rather than side by side, with little distance to overcome. Find a real problem in each place.

For example, it could be a problem for a beleaguered tour guide to avoid the seductive ploys of a hotel manager. If the tour guide plays "to find accommodations," and the hotel manager plays "to fondle the tour guide," this real conflict physicalizes the dialogue.

How can time work as an obstacle?

Whereas many characters face difficult places and events, others face the problem of time running out. They must face a jury, find a job, overcome an illness, get married. Some characters face the last days before their death.

If you are playing a scene in which time is an obstacle, use a timepiece whenever possible. Relate to a watch, sundial, clock, or some form of physical measurement of time at specific moments throughout the scene. Time is an obstacle only if it presents a real problem in a particular place. You've got to get to the church for the wedding, to the airport for that flight, and so on.

How do objects and tasks serve as obstacles?

Objects can easily block your character's action. Imagine the vexation of having to work at an office with a disconnected telephone or to dance at your senior prom in tight shoes. Objects such as a broken window shade, ringing alarm clock, or glaring light increase the adversity of your immediate environment. Think about trying to open a stuck door to escape when an enemy is chasing you. Remember the frustration of having your computer crash as you're trying to type a critical exam paper that's overdue.

In *Dream Girl* (1945), Elmer Rice has written into Georgina's opening monologue a series of frustrating objects.

DREAM GIRL: OBJECTS AS OBSTACLES

Possible Action: To postpone getting up

Possible Obstacles/Objects: Alarm clock, sunlight

Georgina: (*yawning heavily*) Ohhhh! (*Then, angrily, to the alarm clock*) For heaven's sake, will you please shut up? (*She shuts off the alarm clock, then leans over and pulls up an imaginary window shade. The bed is flooded with morning sunlight.* GEORGINA *moans, shakes her head, and stretches her arms*) Oh, dear! Another day! How awful! Who was it that said: "Must we have another day?" Dorothy Parker, I suppose. I wonder if she really says all those things. (*With a sigh*) Well, time to get up, I guess. (*She plumps herself down again and snuggles her head in the pillow*)

A physical task can also create a real problem for your character. A character may need to take deep breaths to calm her nerves without being observed by another, and this presents a real problem.

How can my clothing work as an obstacle?

Your character's clothing can hinder action. Have you ever tried to walk seductively in a business suit or to move gracefully in work boots? Your costume influences all your physical actions. You may cower in too-casual clothing at a ball. You may have difficulty climbing to your seat at a football stadium in high heels or running on the beach in a tight skirt.

Put yourself at risk in rehearsal. For example, if you are playing a homely teacher, wear some of your own tacky clothes, ugly accessories, and no makeup ("oh, no," you say). Find clothing that truly dictates what you do.

Clothing specific to an ailment can drastically restrict movement. Have you ever tried to get dressed with your arm in a sling or to clean house with your leg in a cast?

Physical handicaps create great obstacles. Think of a blind man finding his way with a stick, an athlete hobbling on crutches, a veteran limping with a wooden leg. Many lead roles revolve around impairments: blindness, deafness, muteness, a hunched back, enlarged head, long nose, powerless legs, paralysis.

Can you remember how embarrassed you felt when you clumped down an aisle with a cast on your leg? Or how irritated you became because of a suit that was too tight? Most physical obstacles have some psychological component and vice versa.

What are psychological obstacles?

At the root of our fullest involvement . . . is a deliberate disjunction of impressions, often what we see working against what we hear, or vice versa; often what we feel working against what we think.

J. L. Shyan, *Drama, Stage and Audience*

Psychological obstacles are internal barriers within your character or other characters. Psychological obstacles are mental forces, something disturbing thoughts and thwarting actions. A psychological obstacle can be an idea in your character's mind that hinders what you do. Often it means experiencing another's outlook blocking your actions. You find yourself unable to reach him because of his slanted point of view. You adjust your responses and try to move past resistance. You feel that if this person could only experience your predicament, he would help. For example, a character warns another that he must sell his house. But the other has a problem of being easily distracted. He rambles on about encyclopedias and Paris. Distraction stops the first character from getting the second to focus on this crisis.

Onstage, you often try to influence the point of view of another character. In *Romeo and Juliet*, Romeo must overcome not just the physical obstacle of the balcony but also the psychological one of Juliet's outlook: her fears about her parents' disapproval. His obstacle is her attachment to her parents.

To overcome the psychological obstacle in this scene, Romeo should begin experiencing Juliet's point of view. He would ask himself, "What is she thinking as she looks at me? What is she imagining her parents will say if they walk in right now? Is she picturing her parents locking her up forever?"

Why are psychological obstacles important?

The most vexing obstacles onstage and in life are psychological ones. For example, you can't get another character to understand you, to love you, to support you. You can't pull yourself out of a depression. You can see and accept a locked door, but it's hard to deal with a locked-up personality. Onstage, you try different ways to break through internal barriers.

Onstage, you are often dealing with an obstacle as it presents itself in another actor. You must try to overcome the way that character thinks. Mental barriers incite you to corner the other character to get what you want.

Sometimes a psychological obstacle is actually a second side of yourself. You are fighting against your own disturbing thoughts and feelings. When this happens, be sure to use many details of circumstances to make your thoughts gnaw away at you. Background material strengthens inner obstacles. Using your imagination, fill in the character's present and past with details from your own life and fiction. In the following exercise, mental obstacles of preoccupation pressure the action.

BACKGROUND FOR THREE-MINUTE SEQUENCE

I am an unemployed actress wanting to do something significant in my field, married to a neat, caring husband who has just lost his job.

What time is it?

4:45 P.M. Saturday, May 15, 1991, spring, light breeze outside. I'm wearing summer clothes. Cost of living is skyrocketing (esp. at grocery store) and may inflate with the president's energy plan pending Congress. My in-laws are due shortly for a first visit to our new house.

Where am I?

I am in the children's section of the living room, by the fireplace, in our house in the country town of Lambertville, New Jersey. Tom, my husband, is mowing the lawn, which he has not cut for two weeks. Lambertville is an expensive New York suburb. There are over fifty theaters in a seventy-five-mile radius of Lambertville. We have a mortgage of $820 a month.

My show is ending at Bucks County Playhouse. Everyone gleefully assumes I'll come back and reapply for a company position again. I just opened two rejection letters from theaters because of cutbacks. I cannot act at Bucks County next year. My in-laws loaned us money for buying this house and want us to settle happily here.

What do I want?

Main Objective: To impress Tom's relatives

Immediate (Mental) Objective: To alleviate unemployment problem

ACTION: To clean

Subactions (physical)

1. to put on cleaning gloves, scarf
2. to clean fireplace
3. to dust mantel
4. to dust end table, phone
5. to dust end table, lamp
6. to dust coffee table
7. to clean bookcase
8. to clean chair

Psychological Actions

1. to define what's wrong with my auditioning

What's in my way?

Major Obstacle: Time running out

Other Obstacles: Worry about unemployment problem

anger at presumptuous visit
desire to go to the movies

desire to read and rest before kids come home
damp, muggy afternoon
dislike for physical activity
Tom's neat streak
Tom needs to mow, then clean up
my stomach and nerves
headache
dinner unmade

State of mind

Events

I am discouraged and uneasy; I have constipation, piercing stomach cramps; I hate myself for failures on interviews; I had expected employment at another theater. I am angry about not being able to go to the movies and our surprise in-law visit tonight.

People (in thoughts)

Tom—want to keep his spirits up for tonight and for his job hunt.
Director Richards—want to tell him off for his rude interview.
Producer O—want to play up to him for a small role.
Actor B—want to tell him off for his hypocrisy.

Objects (surrounding me)

Phone—want it to ring and resolve problem.
Rug—want it to return my stock money.
Lamp—want it to take me back to Japan where I was on a fellowship.
Chair (*by phone*)—want money from parents, not gifts.
Sofa and table—want to forget how I had to scrape when married in acting school.
Coffee table—want to forget how Tom searched to find $8 table.
Bookcase—want to forget all work I did to excel; stop being acting student.
TV—want to forget my failure to make money as an actress and dust; want Tom to make more money.

Note: The actress may not think of these thought/obstacles in the same order or use all of them for each performance. She is loading her work with mental obstacles because they are capricious and may vary each performance. All these obstacles distract her from the action of cleaning. Also, during performance, she will not force herself to concentrate on them. The work of recalling and specifying obstacles comes in rehearsal. And the battle is to keep cleaning.

How do psychological obstacles encourage vulnerability?

Stanislavski considered psychological obstacles the most useful and powerful because they are intricately tied to your feelings. Vulnerability, the ability to be wounded easily, is a major trait of good actors. It means you allow your ideas about the other characters and yourself to hurt you. You are continually deepening your interpretation of the problem while trying to overcome it. Good actors transform themselves into vulnerable, unpredictable characters. They intrigue the audience by the range of their adjustments to inner obstacles.

EXERCISES

1. *Handicap Walk.* Walk across the floor as fast as you can, pretending you have a broken ankle. Where is the pain you avoid when you walk? Research different accidents (car crash, a fall from a horse, street fight, ballet mishap) and their psychological ramifications. Rehearse one.

2. *Physical Obstacle List.* Make a list of the physical obstacles (places, events, people) that could have impeded you today from reaching this class.

3. *Physical Obstacle Sequence.* Re-create one of the following: (a) someone writing a paper with a broken pen; (b) someone cooking a meal with the wrong utensils; (c) someone reading without glasses; (d) someone escaping while blindfolded. Concentrate totally on performing the action several times until it becomes organic.

4. *Problem Computer.* Think of several possible problems with a computer: a stuck key, broken space bar, uncooperative mouse. Type a particular term paper pretending you're working against one particular problem.

5. *Blindfolded Breakfast.* Get up and make breakfast while blindfolded. Repeat the exercise in class.

■ REHEARSING OBSTACLES

How can difficult obstacles help me?

Even if you are on the right track, you'll get run over if you just sit there.

Will Rogers

Difficult obstacles focus you totally on the action. The harder it is for you to do something—climb a mountain, make a phone call, unlock a door—the more carefully you'll commit yourself to each choice. Tough obstacles are the best gifts you can give yourself in a scene.

Onstage, your character must make urgent decisions, think quickly, react to some extremely painful pressure. That's one of the reasons why when I coach a scene, I'll say, "Put more pressure on her, make her respond to you. React to what she just said; did you hear that? Yes, repeat it for me, respond to that." Onstage, someone is always forcing another to do something. In my early years of teaching acting, I used to sit back and analyze for about twenty-five minutes what the obstacle was for the actors, and then I'd say, "Come back next class and do that scene," and I would see the same results I saw earlier. But now I referee the scene in class, and when I know the actors are physically experiencing the obstacles, I then step out. Sometimes I'm a devil's advocate, setting up an argument, egging it on, and after it gets ignited, stepping out of it.

How can I strengthen each obstacle?

Strengthen each obstacle by eliminating the phrase "My character is not concerned about this problem" from your vocabulary. Hook yourself into only one option: Your character is more rattled by and determined to overcome the obstacles than you are!

Imagine yourself playing the Commuter in the following opening scene. Ask yourself, "When has someone confronted me like this?" Experience the Man's opposing point of view. Try to recall when you felt suspicious of someone.

Man: Well, I've been meaning to talk to you. I hope you won't mind. I suppose you're an easygoing type and—you missed your train?

Commuter: By not more than a minute. I rush into the station, and it pulls out before my very eyes.

Man: You could have run after it.

Commuter: Of course, it's silly, I know. If I hadn't been loaded down with all those damned packages, bundles, boxes, God knows what else! Like a jackass! But you know women—errands, errands—it never stops! It took me three minutes, believe me, just to get out of the taxi and get my fingers through all those strings, two packages to a finger.

Man: You must have been quite a sight. You know what I'd have done? I'd have left them in the cab.

Commuter: And my wife? Oh, yes! And my daughters? And all their friends?

Man: Let them scream. I'd enjoy it enormously.

Commuter: That's because you probably have no idea what women are like when they get to the country in the summer!

Man: But of course I know. Precisely because I do know. (*a pause*) They all begin by saying they won't really need anything.

(from Luigi Pirandello's *The Man with the Flower in His Mouth*, 1926; translated by William Murray, 1970)

Ask yourself, "What stranger from my life would I have difficulty overcoming? What could I personally risk losing to this man?" For example, a missed train could unnerve you if you are unarmed, carrying your paycheck, and confronting a drug addict. What's at stake? Possibly your life.

Study the play! Better to have too many obstacles than too few. The more your character has to lose, the more suspenseful the obstacle. For example, in a tragedy, his life is what a character has to lose. In a comedy, you might risk something vital to you like all your money, if you're greedy, or your looks, if you're vain. Remember in rehearsals to give yourself the right to experiment, to play, and to fail. Often you must go past the mark to find the limits imposed by the obstacles.

■ CHECKLIST

1. What is my major obstacle? Who is doing this to me?
2. What little obstacles are stopping me moment to moment?
3. How are the place, time, and events stopping me?
4. How are the other characters hindering me?

■ FINAL PROJECTS

1. *Progressive Exercise.* This exercise is related to the ones in chapters 1 and 2, so you have the same partner. Rehearse this sequence several times.

   EXERCISE 3:   An empty church or synagogue. Two more years have passed. You and your partner are intensely related. You each play an opposing action and objective, and each has one main obstacle in the sequence. One of you has a physical handicap, and one has a professional handicap.
      Each of you should make up background information to support a total commitment to overcoming this main obstacle. Include all the information learned heretofore. Many minor obstacles may also affect you in the scene. Begin the scene in silence, with each of you engaged in a physical activity. Then one of you should begin the verbal conflict. Hand in your written background for the exercise.

2. *Hardheaded Monologue.* Rehearse a monologue that you are addressing to someone else. Identify actions to overcome

the other person's point of view. Determine your major action, objective, and obstacle. Allow minor obstacles to affect you momentarily throughout the sequence. Hand in your written homework on the exercise.

3. *Lost Object.* Re-create a sequence with objects in which you have one major action (to hunt), one physical obstacle (something hidden), and one objective (to find it). Make up background information that puts you at great risk because of the lost object. Rehearse in a familiar place with someone actually hiding the object from you. Then re-create the sequence in class. Hand in a written account of your background and of your plan for the scene's actions, objectives, and mental and physical obstacles.

4. *Opposing Dreams.* Pick a partner and set up a scene in which your needs are in total conflict. Pick a place that stirs up the conflict for you. Make sure the conflict is something you develop out of your personal convictions. A conflict might be that I want to move to New York because I am an actress, and you want me to stay in the Midwest so you can go into the cattle business. Between rehearsals, get to know and like your partner by doing something together—going to lunch, to the park, to the movies—that appears unrelated to the scene. Use this real memory of when you got along to make you want to overcome the distance you now feel. Hand in your written homework on the exercise.

4

INNER IMAGES
What motivates my action?

This chapter evaluates the use of sources from your own life that stimulate the character's action.

As an actor, you enter the field out of this intense desire to make a contribution, to do something very fine in the art world, to use your pain, anguish, and life experience to lighten the load or make someone else's perceptions keener. You want the human race to advance out of your sacrifice of yourself because at least 50 percent of what you relive onstage is *very painful.* Even in comedy it's somewhat painful to intensely remember things that are already gone.

Joe Warfield, actor

■ WHAT IS AN INNER IMAGE?

An inner image is a picture flashing before your mind's eye. In life, you operate from an incessant stream of images. Inner images running through your head color how you think and react to each situation. Some images influence you momentarily. A ring may remind you of a friend's engagement, graduation, or death. Haunting images may have an intense and/or constant effect on your psyche and thus on your actions.

Both actors and characters experience inner images. Onstage, you try to find images from your life that are similar to ones the character might have. Many inner images can create a charged mental state. For example, a character might literally shrink from thoughts of her mother's boyfriends.

Actors describe inner images as substitutions, personal sources, or inner objects. *Substitutions* means images from your life that replace each thought of the character. When putting words on paper, the playwright envisioned a complete character with an active mind. Fabricating personal images for things mentioned onstage helps you develop the mind-set to react as the character.

The inner image alters your state of being, what you're actually experiencing.

Why are inner images important?

Inner images root you in the character's experience while at the same time connecting you with your own impulses. Like an electric current, they spark your actions. In *Romeo and Juliet,* for example, if Juliet contacts her image of some unattainable lover (possibly the actor playing Romeo) right before she says the line "O Romeo, Romeo! wherefore art thou Romeo?" that connection will inspire the action "to lament." Similarly, the memory of a velvet-textured rose might stimulate the action of another line, "That which we call a rose by any other name would smell as sweet."

Your images charge your performance, especially your dialogue. In physical action scenes, actors may give inner images less focus, but in highly verbal scenes, actors must intensify inner images. The voice beams from a source of inner images, and no matter how perfect the outer instrument, it will not be effective if the power is disconnected. If you are physically wrestling with another onstage, you rehearse a pattern of physical moves. If you are wrestling with your thoughts, you fight a pattern of images. Onstage, you may evoke, then fight, something as intangible as a series of memories and sensations. The more inner images motivating a role, the less you will feel the need to always be "acting."

In the "Bus Observation" chart that follows, the actor has noted inner images that will intensify her actions. The images are idiosyncratic and cryptic, but filled with personal meaning for the actor. You, too, have certain memories and mental pictures that stir your actions.

BUS OBSERVATION

Scene: A bus in New Orleans

Main Obstacle: Driver's indifference

ACTION	OBJECTIVE	OBSTACLE	INNER IMAGE
1. to hurry onto the bus	to win approval from the driver	slippery floor	Hertz airport van
2. to slug change into the fare box	to win approval	thin coin slot	clogged streetcar slot
3. to look for twenty more cents	to win approval	empty wallet	dirty Indian nickels
4. to scramble inside my bag	to stall the driver	papers in bag	secret pouch in black bag
5. to dump out my wallet	to stall	many wallet photos	high school photos
6. to moan	to soften the driver	no time	spinal chart
7. to rub my back	to soften	heavy topcoat	Dr. Lewis's pills
8. to check my pockets	to soften	pockets full	stitched pockets
9. to wave my eviction notice	to overcome the driver	other passengers' impatience	Magazine Street rental note

ACTION	OBJECTIVE	OBSTACLE	INNER IMAGE
10. to droop my shoulders	to overcome	driver's indifference	Daddy's sad shoulders
11. to ransack my bag	to overcome	messy bag	pencils, pens, writing supplies
12. to slam more change into box	to punish the driver	broken fare box	Grandma Nix's noisy money box
13. to knife the driver with a dirty look	to punish	driver's indifference	Mother Johnson's expression
14. to stride down the aisle	to pulverize the driver	unsteadiness	Blue Ribbon award

Why should I keep inner images secret?

Although you should write your substitutions down, do not tell the other actors and artists what sources you are using. Concealing your substitutions enhances their mystery, heightens others' concentration, and will ultimately fortify yours. Remember, you and the other actors need to believe in what you're doing onstage. Secrecy encourages your sense of truth.

Some directors impose secrecy. In one play in which an argument about fixing a flat tire took place, the director took two actors out into the parking lot and made them actually change a tire, then swore them to secrecy. Whenever they got to that spot in the play, that real secret bonded them together, creating an extraordinary spark.

How do I contact useful images?

Contacting useful inner images is easy. It requires just the openness to connect with your past experiences. Your procedures need make sense only to you. Nobody has to know what is going on inside your head! Imagine yourself talking to a fortune-teller who calls up fantasies from your life. Sometimes you'll have to embrace troubling images, and even mental discomfort. Creating inner images for a role for the first time can be as challenging as lifting weights. Keep contacting different sources, and powerful ones will eventually take hold.

Why is relaxation the first step?

Relaxation helps you develop the concentration needed to focus on an imaginary world. It readies your mind and body for suggestion. Start with vocal and physical warm-ups, or practice controlling your breathing. Find a quiet place, sit in a comfortable position, and pay attention to your breath flowing in and out for at least twenty minutes. Focus within yourself. Some people find peace in the moment between the inhale and exhale; they feel in perfect harmony with themselves. Through quiet meditation, you can relax and gradually reawaken your inner self. When you find that center of being, you will know that you already possess all the resources needed for any moment onstage.

How should I rehearse?

In rehearsals, allow images associated with the words of your dialogue to surface and to stir your emotions. Develop points of reference from your own life for every person, place, or thing related to, talked about, or listened to onstage.

Let your body experience the lines; observe what feelings come up; discover what images stimulate your feelings. Although most actors contact images through the sense of sight, in some scenes other senses predominate, such as when hearing a mournful tune, smelling an enticing scent, feeling the texture of a loved one's skin. External stimuli such as lighting effects, sound effects, costumes, and furniture can also heighten substitutions and enrich your inner life.

How can inner images help me make an entrance?

Calling upon inner images can help you make a strong entrance. Determine your character's state of mind before you enter. What inner images lead you to the initial action? If after entering your character must reprimand a friend, you would do it differently depending on what thoughts are going through your head. To contact inner images for your entrance, ask yourself, "How am I feeling right now?" In *Building a Character* Stanislavski wrote: "At any moment, you could contact many different emotional states, such as you're concerned, cold, hungry, distracted, sad, tired, lonely. Allow one of them to lure you into what the character is experiencing. This stream of images, fed by all sorts of fictitious inventions, given circumstances, puts life into a role."

Knowing that you have to perform intensifies your inner life. All of a sudden, you start to vibrate with more energy, focus, and attention. For some actors, it's as if someone is holding a gun to them saying they're going to die any second. It heightens their awareness.

What is an inner monologue?

An inner monologue is a silent conversation with yourself as the character. It helps you activate your character's stream of consciousness. Some actors use an inner monologue to keep inner images flowing. They verbalize responses going on in the mind while the action is occurring. For example, if another character reveals your secret, you might say to yourself: "Oh, my God, I didn't know he knew that!"

In an inner monologue you are evaluating what the other character does—every facial gesture, sound, pause, breathing pattern—before responding. Notice how you talk to yourself, how angry you are, because of what you are seeing. Listen to yourself in rehearsal. Test different associations that stir your thoughts.

For example, one character's inner monologue upon arriving at her married sister's tiny apartment after a long, tiring journey might be: "I sure could use some bourbon to calm my nerves. Gosh, the place is a dump and so small. Where's the booze? What's that smell? Cigarettes. Oh, I was afraid he smoked! Disgusting. Well, I'd better keep quiet. I'm broke, and I don't want him to throw me out! God, what a tiny little place. I hope they don't make love every night—loudly. The walls are paper thin."

What is an inner problem?

In your inner monologue you may address your character's inner problem, the concern that agitates you in a sequence. Even if your character is worried about something pleasant, such as which dress to wear to a party, you operate from a dissatisfaction onstage. Sometimes a character may search out loud for a resolution to the problem. At other times, the character may not verbalize the problem. For example, even though the topic of betrayal is never mentioned, a character may leave someone at the close of the scene. But because betrayal is what leads to the departure, the actor needs to work against this inner problem all along.

Channel your images toward the inner problem of the character. For example, my character's inner problem might be insecurity. I begin with the thought "I am (picture my new car outside) indifferent about this workshop because I am (hand trembling) afraid I will do poorly and don't want to (stained white dress) embarrass myself." Notice how contacting images helped me move from indifference to insecurity.

What are sense memory and emotional memory?

Sensory work re-creates the context of the emotion. Build a house, and the emotion will return to live there again.

Dale Moffit, actor training specialist, Southern Methodist University

An inner image is often a relived memory. Sense memory is a technique for reliving physical sensations; certain inner images can trigger them: a sweaty forehead, labored breathing, a raspy throat, a pounding heart. Notice which image triggers which sensation.

For instance, the memory of hot tennis shoes on the pavement brings back the oppressive heat of summer; the image of a sandy beach evokes the prickly sensation to your feet; recalling the sound of dry wind screaming over the water makes you experience that wind in your face. Reliving a detail of a past event can stimulate memory and help you relive a particular sensation. Onstage, you may have to experience such things as a sudden chill or high fever throughout a scene. To do so, you will contact and respond to one or more images through sense memory.

Emotional memory is a technique for reliving a detail of a past event to evoke a feeling, such as sadness. Try recalling an experience similar to one in the script, as it happened, with all the physical details. When an event in a scene arouses feelings, note the specific item that stirs them. That trigger lets you make an instantaneous connection with the moment. For example, to grieve over a friend's death, you might try to remember moments when you enjoyed him. Remember the time, the weather, the colors. Hear the sounds, see what you saw, feel the temperature. Find the precise images that evoke an emotion.

In the following description, one actor recalls a time when she cried at a hospital in order to evoke a feeling of sadness. "I am in a hospital waiting room with my mother, and images of my father's heart surgery are making me cry. For example, I see my father's lifeless hand on the operating table, feel the pressure of the doctor's fingers, hear the lilt of the nurse's voice, then smell the cold antiseptic aroma. As these images of my father on the operating table flash to mind, my throat dries up, I feel a lump in my chest."

Let me emphasize, first, that not everyone can use the technique of emotional memory, and it sometimes requires strict supervision. Second, it is largely a rehearsal technique. In performance, an actor should not abandon the circumstances of the play and substitute specific emotional scenes from his own life because this destroys any hope of a through line of action. You infuse the character's present with your experience, but you must stay with your action onstage!

■ SENDING INNER IMAGES

How do I send inner images?

After you know how to reexperience powerful images, you must learn how to send them to someone else. Sending inner images means provoking another person to experience them. Send your images to another character by concentrating on getting them across through the words. Before speaking, you visualize mental pictures, which your words then reflect.

For example, another character could interpret the following sentence many ways, depending on the inner images you used: "That farmer should not be allowed behind the garage near the chicken coop." Some examples of subtext, the hidden images you use to give the words meaning, for the line include:

1. A pervert doing strange sensual things behind an empty shed

2. A robust planter approaching a minefield of bombs in a village shack

3. A chicken thief disguised as a farmer slipping into a forbidden area

Make sure that when you send your words to another character, she not only understands the meaning of your lines, but also sees what you see in your mind's eye while you are speaking. If you focus on communicating your images, you will contact not only the other character but also the audience.

Remember, you cannot simultaneously be in your own world and look into someone else's eyes—you can't focus within and without at the same time. Inner images stop when you direct your attention to outer things.

EXERCISES

1. *Recitation.* Recite to a partner the details of your daily behavior. Note that you cannot simultaneously recall events and retain active eye contact with your partner. You need to look inward at specific images, if just for a second, before speaking directly to the partner.

2. *Recalling Events.* Right now, make a list of ten things you did last night. Notice how you have to look inward before writing down each thought.

   1. _____
   2. _____
   3. _____
   4. _____
   5. _____
   6. _____
   7. _____
   8. _____
   9. _____
   10. _____

3. *The Entrance.* Practice entering and answering the telephone by just saying "Hello." Visualize five inner images as you go to pick up the receiver. Notice the series of images that influences you the most. Stage three ways to say "Hello" based on different inner images.

4. *Crisis Monologue.* Practice a monologue in which you are in total inner conflict. Note: Load your words with personal associations to evoke inner images.

5. *Inner Problem.* Choose a strong inner problem based on dire circumstances to relate to while doing a physical task that is now a habit to you.

Why should I check my partner?

Check your partner to assess how your inner images are being received. She should be responding *while* you are speaking and vice versa. Don't make the mistake of letting the end of the preceding speech stimulate your lines; find the loaded words *inside* the speech that excite your responses. In many sequences, especially fight scenes, you may actually need to overlap the ending of another's line to keep the momentum going.

Experiment with pauses. Use them sparingly and make "X" marks in your script where you stop to evaluate whether the other character is listening. Generally, pauses work best inside a series of lines. Notice how in the following exchange, a pause before Brack's line "No!" would slow down the momentum of the conflict, but a pause in the middle of the line could create suspense.

Hedda: —so they found him there?

Brack: Yes. With a fired gun in his pocket. Mortally wounded.

Hedda: Yes—in the chest.

Brack: (*no pause*) No! (*Pause*)—in the guts.

Especially important at the beginning of a scene, pauses provide the listener space to understand your thoughts. Make a conscious effort to set up a few psychological pauses so that the other character receives the images you are sending. But don't overdo them. Long pauses are not necessarily significant. You've got to earn pauses by speaking fast most of the time.

■ CHECKLIST

1. Am I contacting exciting inner images?

2. Am I relaxed enough to induce vivid thoughts?

3. What inner monologue is controlling my thoughts?

4. Am I using inner images to make my entrance and exit? To move the other characters?

■ FINAL PROJECTS

1. *Progressive Exercise.* This exercise is related to the one in chapters 1–5, so you have the same partner. Rehearse this sequence several times.

> **EXERCISE 4:** A bumpy airplane. Two more years have passed. You and your partner are intensely related. You each play a strong action with an objective and obstacle. One of you has a professional handicap and one a physical handicap.
>
> Each of you should tap your past to find a vivid series of inner images. Each of you has an inner problem that never comes up in the scene. Include all the information learned heretofore.
>
> Begin the scene in silence with each of you engaged in a physical activity. Then one of you should begin the verbal conflict. Hand in your written work on the exercise.

2. *Inner Monologue.* Rehearse a short, two-person scene and concentrate on letting inner images flow freely before your mind's eye. After saying each line, describe under your breath what you are experiencing. What is your mood as you observe your thoughts, feelings, and sensations? Test different associations that might connect to your lines to uncover meaningful inner images. Practice the scene again and observe what the other character does during the scene—every facial gesture, sound, pause, breathing pattern—before responding. Describe everything in an inner monologue. Actually write out the inner monologue as spoken. Stage the final version in class.

3. *Subtext.* Fill in explosive inner images for a scene. Notice which areas have the greatest lack of images, then rerun the scene, focusing on those sections. Stage the scene.

Try the experiment of having one actor keep to the text, while the other actor speaks not only the text but also all the thoughts that come to mind during the scene. The second "text," made up of the actor's thoughts, may sometimes co-incide with the words, but the actors should not let this confuse them. Rather, they should discover that two conversations are going on in the scene—the text and the thoughts of the characters.

4. *Sense Memory.* Make up an inner image chart, divided into positives and negatives, for sight, hearing, smell, touch, and taste. For each of the senses, list five things that you really love (such as a fifty-foot spruce Christmas tree) and five that you hate (such as your dog's vomit). Notice how contacting each image makes you feel.

Five Senses Chart

SENSE	POSITIVE EXAMPLES	NEGATIVE EXAMPLES
Sight	1. _____	1. _____
	2. _____	2. _____
	3. _____	3. _____
	4. _____	4. _____
	5. _____	5. _____
Hearing	1. _____	1. _____
	2. _____	2. _____
	3. _____	3. _____
	4. _____	4. _____
	5. _____	5. _____
Smell	1. _____	1. _____
	2. _____	2. _____
	3. _____	3. _____

	4. _____	4. _____
	5. _____	5. _____
Taste	1. _____	1. _____
	2. _____	2. _____
	3. _____	3. _____
	4. _____	4. _____
	5. _____	5. _____
Touch	1. _____	1. _____
	2. _____	2. _____
	3. _____	3. _____
	4. _____	4. _____
	5. _____	5. _____

5. *Emotional Memory.* Review every month of the past two years for an important inner image and make a list. Initially you may remember just certain surroundings—the wallpaper in your room or a picture on the wall—but by contacting them, your memories will grow. Allow this experience to encourage you to keep a daily record of your impressions. When appropriate, hand in your list.

6. *Singing Shakespeare.* Stage a one-page Shakespearean sequence or a sonnet. Then perform it with you and a classmate singing the lines back and forth. Contact vivid images to support you in singing out Shakespeare. This technique helps you focus inward, then fire information powerfully on the phrase, as in song.

5
THE SCORE
How do I chart
what I'm doing?

This chapter describes a written record that helps to reinforce
your actions by clarifying your choices each moment onstage.

There is still that mystery of an actor who can repeat every detail because
of his work and his life. The best actors try the most things in rehearsal.
They are never satisfied, always looking for more adjustments and retaining
them, and therefore in performance they achieve the greatest heights.

Gilles Gleizes, French director

■ WHAT IS A SCORE?

A score is a written account you keep of how to play a role. It
assists you in layering complexity into your acting. Like a mu-
sician's sheet music, your score charts the combinations you
play. It solidifies the rehearsal process. At home, you study the
play, fantasize about the role, and note choices already determined in rehearsal. At the next rehearsal, you re-create choices
and open yourself to more inspiration. A strong score provides
clarity and precision. It involves testing certain possibilities
and choosing to play fully a particular course. A good score
helps you store details in your unconscious, so when performing you can react spontaneously. It provides you with the
specifics to re-create any moment you've originally found.

How do I write a score?

To write an exciting score, you need the ability to transcribe accurately what you do. Although scores may vary from actor to actor, an effective score usually captures the elements of conflict for each act, scene, beat, and line of the role. It isolates the action (What am I doing?), the objective (What do I want?), the obstacle (What's in my way?), and the inner image (What's my personal source?). Some actors record actions, objectives, obstacles, inner images in the margins. Some note objectives in big print and actions in small print. Most abbreviate inner images to conceal personal substitutions. Many actors make a chart of all the elements of conflict and use it as a checklist opposite each page of text.

How does the score keep my acting in shape?

The score provides the structure for a physical and mental workout for you as the character. That's why this book was written: to guide you effortlessly through a routine for developing your finest performance.

A score—like your background homework—will increase your self-confidence and your ability to get work earlier in your career. You may skirt much of the frustration of rejection. You may be paid to act rather than to do other work that would distract you from your art!

Who first used the term "score"?

Stanislavski first used the term "score." He said we should call this long catalogue of minor and major objectives, units, scenes, and acts the *score of a role.*

> . . . One can call them natural objectives. There can be no doubt that such a score, based on such objectives, will draw the actor—physically speaking—closer to the real action of his part. (It) . . . stirs the action actor to physical action.
>
> The first requirement is that the score have the power to attract . . . excite the actor not only by its external physical truth

but above all by its inner beauty. . . . Let us now add depth to the
score. . . . The difference will lie in the inner life . . . inner impulses, psychological intimations . . . that constitute the inner
tone. . . . We can experience varying emotions when playing a
score with the same objectives but in different keys . . . quiet or
joyful . . . sad or . . . disturbed or in an excited key. . . . One's score
which is to portray human passions, must be rich, colorful, and
varied. . . . An actor must know the nature of a passion . . . how
to cull (from the text) the component units, objectives, moments, which in their sum total add up to a human passion. . . .
The score saturates every particle of an actor's inner being. . . .
In this innermost . . . core . . . all the remaining objectives con-
verge as it were, into super objective . . . the concentration of
the entire score. . . . For the actor the through action is the
active attainment of the super objective. (*An Actor's Handbook* by Constantin Stanislavski, edited and translated by Elizabeth Reynolds Hapgood, Theatre Arts Books, New York, 1963,
pp. 124–125)

■ FINDING THE ELEMENTS

The important thing is not to stop questioning.

Albert Einstein

How do I find my super objective?

The most important element in the score is the super objective
of your role. A super objective is an overall aim. Writing a score
begins with finding the purpose, or super objective, of the play.
It's the playwright's vision that drove him to write the play. Ask
yourself, "Why did the playwright write this story? What aim
motivated her creation of these events?" The super objective of
the play contains its meaning. Read the play many times to discover its super objective. Better still, try to fall in love with the
play, so you feel it in your bones. Read the play as if you are living through it.

Certain super objectives, especially those about love and money, drive many plays. Some popular super objectives include "to save someone," "to kill someone," "to marry someone," "to punish someone," "to get rich off someone," "to protect someone."

Understanding the super objective of the play will help you relate to the super objective of your character. This burning passion motivates each action and propels you through the play. As you reread the script, you will begin to sense your character's fundamental need. Like a magnet, your super objective draws you toward major objectives from scene to scene.

How do I score major objectives?

To score major objectives, write down the specific goal you want to achieve at the top of each sequence. This major objective is always blocked—usually by the major objective of another character.

Tennessee Williams's *Suddenly Last Summer* is about a young woman, Catharine, who is about to have a lobotomy. The play runs on the super objective "to save Catharine." In scene 1, Mrs. Venable wants to get the doctor to quiet her niece with a lobotomy. Dr. Cukrowicz tries to persuade her to support nonsurgical treatment. By the end of the scene, the collision of their major objectives has created the play's first crisis. Notice the doctor's major objective running beneath the following lines.

SUDDENLY LAST SUMMER

Doctor's Major Objective: To get her to forbid surgery

Doctor: (*quietly*) My God. (*Pause*)—Mrs. Venable, suppose after meeting the girl and observing the girl and hearing this story she babbles—I still shouldn't feel that her condition's—intractable enough! to justify the risks of—suppose I shouldn't feel that nonsurgical treatment such as insulin shock and electric shock and—.

Mrs. Venable: SHE'S HAD ALL THAT AT SAINT MARY'S! Nothing else is left for her.

How do I score immediate or line-by-line objectives?

A major objective provokes a series of immediate needs from beat to beat. If your major objective is "to make someone love you," the first goal is "to get a date," the second is "to get a kiss." Immediate objectives are these specific, even line-by-line aims that emotionally charge the score. By naming them, you start to store them in your unconscious.

Because of their momentary nature, you are more likely to forget immediate objectives. Write them down in pencil so you can make adjustments as rehearsals progress and new discoveries are made. Let me emphasize, there is nothing wrong with a repeated objective when varied actions are tried to accomplish it. Repeated actions, however, run the risk of boring the audience. Avoid them unless the repetition makes an important dramatic point.

In the following scene (act 4, scene 2) from O'Neill's *Ah, Wilderness!* Muriel "wants to enrapture Richard." Notice how the actress has jotted down immediate objectives for certain lines. She might enter wanting "to attract Richard," but after she gets that, she might play "to wound him for ignoring her." Then, perhaps, she tries "to arouse him."

AH, WILDERNESS!: MURIEL'S SCORE

Notes: Role of Muriel

Major Action: To flirt

Scene Tag: Flirting on the Beach

Super Objective: To win Richard

Major Objective: To enrapture

Spine: To seduce

ACTIONS		IMMEDIATE OBJECTIVES
	(*Just now she is in a great thrilled state of timid adventurousness. She hesitates in the shadow at the foot of the path, waiting for* RICHARD *to see her; but he resolutely goes on whistling with back turned, and she has to call him*)	
1. to warn	Muriel: [1]Oh, Dick. Richard: (*turns around with an elaborate simulation of being disturbed*	1. to attract

Immediate objectives	Dialogue	Major objectives
	in the midst of profound meditation) Oh, hello. Is it nine already? Gosh, times passes—when you're thinking.	
2. to admonish 3. to blame	Muriel: (*coming toward him as far as the edge of the shadow—disappointedly*)[2] I thought you'd be waiting right here at the end of the path.[3] I'll bet you'd forgotten I was even coming.	2. to wound 3. to wound
	Richard: (*strolling a little toward her but not too far—carelessly*) No, I hadn't forgotten, honest. But I got to thinking about life.	
4. to goad 5. to coo 6. to tease 7. to whisper	Muriel: [4]You might think of me for a change, after all the risks I've run to see you! (*Hesitating timidly on the edge of the shadow*)[5] Dick! [6]You come here to me.[7] I'm afraid to go out in that bright moonlight where anyone might see me.	4. to arouse 5. to arouse 6. to arouse 7. to arouse
	Richard: (*coming to her—scornfully*) Aw, there you go again— always scared of life!	
8. to criticize 9. to demonstrate 10. to remind	Muriel: (*indignantly*) [8]Dick Miller, I do think you've got an awful nerve to say that after all the risks I've run [9]making this date and then sneaking out! [10]You didn't take the trouble to sneak any letter to me, I notice!	8. to disarm 9. to disarm 10. to disarm

Note in this score the occasional contradiction between immediate objectives and major objectives. For example, "to wound" (immediate objective) appears incongruent with "to enrapture" (major objective). Such inconsistencies linking the thread of the through line ultimately strengthen the impact of the major objective.

What is a through line or spine?

Just as your character is driven by a super objective, your performance is driven by a through line of action, the main thing you do to achieve the objective. The through line is often referred to as the spine of the role because it supports your performance, running from the beginning to the end of the play.

The spine is the track your character pursues to reach his destination. It is composed of the many small actions you perform scene by scene, all oriented in the direction of your super objective. If the play is well written, the spine of your actions will become apparent early on in scoring them.

In *A Streetcar Named Desire*, Stanley Kowalski's spine is brute force. He has run the streets most of his life. This rough quality permeates his every action—how he behaves with his wife, with his friends, with his pretentious sister-in-law, Blanche. His bestiality intimidates Blanche. Because she has been raised in a mansion, never cooked a meal, made a bed, or traveled alone, she recoils when shaking Stanley's dirty hand. The following chart shows how a director has determined that the spine of Stanley is "to bully" and that of Blanche "to enchant."

NOTES FROM *ROGET'S THESAURUS:* THE SPINE

Stanley/strength: powerful, forceful, physical, brutal, lustful, stamina, nerve, virile, muscular; spine = to *bully?*

Blanche/fragility: sensitive, tact, frail, nice, dainty, exact, delicate, discriminating, fastidious; spine = to *enchant?*

How does scoring clarify my major action?

The scoring process helps you relate to your major action in a scene as part of your spine. Notice in the example from *Ah, Wilderness!* how the actress playing Muriel has identified her major action "to flirt" and her spine "to seduce Richard." A certain number of major actions recur in scripts. Giving each scene a tag such as "Flirting on the Beach" reminds you of your major action.

Why do I need to note line-by-line actions?

Each major action is composed of smaller line-by-line actions. Scoring, for the most part, is jotting down line-by-line actions. Changing action holds interest. For example, in the *Ah, Wilderness!* beach scene, Muriel's major action is "to flirt." Within this overall action, Muriel could use several tactics. First, she might warn her boyfriend, next she might admonish him for a past decision, then she might blame him. Muriel might also play actions such as "to wail," "to groan," and "to complain," actions resulting in nonverbal sounds—grunts, moans, sighs, intakes of air.

Along with the actions beneath lines and sounds, observe gestures, your blocking, and stage directions for possible line-by-line actions. Some playwrights offer no stage directions; others, such as O'Neill, specify them as vital clues to the character. Keep yourself open to all possible options for actions.

How do I discover line-by-line actions for characters from different periods?

Discovering actions for characters in different historical periods may require outside reading. Begin by trying to clarify what you are doing. Many things that are described or said may be unclear to you.

Obstacles must be noted in any score because they stimulate variety. When you say an actor is boring, you mean she repeats the same wooden choices. Obstacles provide an easy way to offset predictability. They make you yearn to play different actions by impeding what you are currently doing.

Use the score to strengthen obstacles' possibilities. Which ones are the most effective? Which excite the greatest interest? After discovering your main obstacle, note how you break down minor ones. Obstacles encourage transitions—you disregard a specific line of action and substitute another. In rehearsal, test a range of obstacles because you can always eliminate choices.

How do I find obstacles with my score?

To find obstacles, strengthen the opposition in each scene. Discover the elements stopping you from reaching someone. Work to move that other character and jot down what you are overcoming. Search for obstacles that frustrate your action. For example, should your character throw a pebble to get another's attention? Practice the option of standing far away from him and see whether the obstacle of distance strengthens your action. Strong obstacles will agitate your thoughts and provoke a series of powerful inner images.

Should I score my inner images?

Absolutely! Sufficient inner images will keep your actions motivated. Sometimes you'll forget your inner images in a performance. One night you'll be so excited, and everything will be going perfectly. Then the next night, you'll dry up completely and wonder: "What is it I thought about that made it so interesting before?" So you must jot down the mental pictures that create the sparks. Remember, even when a character commits the most hideous crimes, you can find inner images that unite you. Keep sensitizing yourself to whatever makes you believe in your actions, and write them down.

Should I score every line?

Sometimes a student will ask: "I don't have to score each line, do I? Four different lines in my scene are the same." No, scoring doesn't have to change for every line. But in any interpretation, you should explore every possible nuance.

The more you break down the action, the more expressive you become because of the variety you are generating. Have you ever heard a pianist trill a note? You could play it "bong bong," but "brrrremmm" is more interesting! So I encourage actors to score not only lines, but also pauses, gestures, and sounds.

The most important part of a score is your actions because a range of actions makes you compelling to watch. You express meaning through the little things you are doing with your hands, with your feet, with your body, and with your face. Obstacles, inner images, and objectives affect the little doings, and the score records them, on paper and in your unconscious. In performance, you react spontaneously, like a master pianist gliding through a concerto without sheet music.

■ SCORING AND REHEARSING

Every composer knows the anguish and despair occasioned by forgetting ideas which one has not had the time to write down.

Victor Hugo, nineteenth-century playwright

How can rehearsals help me score?

A score is easiest to record while you are in rehearsal, in the discovery mode. As you test adjustments, simply jot down the strongest ones. You are clarifying choices—something most actors do automatically. Begin on the simplest level, to accumulate your action, objective, obstacle, and inner image. Then further break down each sequence after you determine more detail.

Slow down and absorb what is going on around you! Experience the choices one by one in the progress of your role. Test vivid choices (actions, objectives, obstacles, inner images). Notice moments when the other character responds the way you want. Update and delete items from your score as your interpretation develops. Practice the script in tiny chunks and in bold run-throughs to experience the vitality behind your score.

How can a thesaurus help me add range to the score?

Using a thesaurus when you are foggy about a moment can help you clarify choices. Note the synonyms for the following elements. Each presents a slightly different variation of the moment. Which of the words affects you the most? Which do you fear playing? Why? Which could be the "hot" choice for you?

ACTION	OBJECTIVE	OBSTACLE	INNER IMAGE
1. to teach	1. to inspire you	1. deaf	1. Judy at dominoes
2. to instruct	2. to excite you	2. outside noise	2. Harry at Audubon Park
3. to guide	3. to arouse you	3. you completely lack power to hear	3. algebra II test
4. to counsel	4. to enliven you	4. your unwillingness to hear	4. Ms. Tate at cafeteria
5. to discipline	5. to invigorate you	5. your determination not to listen	5. Newton's car garage

Describe each action, objective, obstacle, and inner image with exciting terminology. As you work on meaning and experiment with detail, you will find yourself effortlessly memorizing your dialogue.

What is a prompt book?

To allow space for scoring, many actors keep a notebook or journal, which they refer to as a "prompt book." Use a three-ring or spring binder so you can keep loose paper for notes and the script itself in the same binder. Make two copies of the script, pasting each page in the center of an $8\frac{1}{2} \times 11$-inch sheet. Place a blank sheet after each page of script. On this scoring page, make columns for action, objective, obstacle, and inner images. In the script next to the first line, write the number 1, referring to number 1 on the opposite scoring page. For each particular line or moment, jot down the action, objective, obstacle, and inner image used. Choose direct infinitive phrases for the actions and objectives.

The following three tables are semiadvanced acting scores. They demonstrate your goal: capturing intuitive ingredients of conflict in print.

THE GLASS MENAGERIE, SCENE 7: LAURA'S SCORE

(JIM *knocks glass horse off table. Music fades.*)

Laura: [121] Oh, it doesn't matter—

Jim: (*picks horse up*) We knocked the little glass horse over.

Laura: [122] Yes.

Jim: (*hands unicorn to* LAURA) Is he broken?

Laura: [123] Now he's just like all the other horses.

Jim: You mean he lost his—?

Laura: [124] He's lost his horn. [125] It doesn't matter. [126] Maybe it's a blessing in disguise.

Jim: Gee, I bet you'll never forgive me. I bet that was your favorite piece of glass.

Laura: [127] Oh, I don't have favorites—(*Pause*) [128] much. [129] It's no tragedy. [130] Glass breaks so easily. [131] No matter how careful you are. [132] The traffic jars the shelves and things fall off them.

Jim: Still, I'm awfully sorry that I was the cause of it.

Laura: [133] I'll just imagine he had an operation. [134] The horn was removed to make him feel less—[135] freakish! (*Crosses L., sits on small table*) [136] Now he will feel more at home with the other horses, the ones who don't have horns. . . .

Super objective: To marry Jim

Spine: To please

Major Obstacle: Shyness

Main Action: To befriend

Scene Tag: Befriending the unicorn

ACTION	OBJECTIVE	OBSTACLE	INNER IMAGE
121. to convince self	to hide feelings	broken favorite	broken swan

122.	to acknowledge	to hide feelings	Jim did it	broken mouse
123.	to examine	to observe break	darkness	sharp edges
124.	to appraise	to state damage	hurt feelings	sharp edges
125.	to convince self	to comfort self	hurt feelings	dirty rag doll
126.	to convince self	to ignore upset	truly upset	swallow hard
127.	to lie	to comfort Jim	truly upset	porcelain angel
128.	to qualify	to let truth escape	reserved feelings	porcelain angel
129.	to excuse	to comfort	the tragedy	suicide
130.	to excuse	to lessen importance	its importance	shards
131.	to assume carefulness	to lessen importance	not being careful	splinters
132.	to simplify	to comfort	both upset	bull in china shop
133.	to fantasize	to comfort	both upset	castoff
134.	to fantasize	to recover	the tragedy	castoff
135.	to improve	to encourage	the tragedy	crippled unicorn
136.	to praise	to delight	the tragedy	medieval tapestry

"VISITOR FROM HOLLYWOOD," *PLAZA SUITE* BY NEIL SIMON: MURIEL'S SCORE

(*When the door opens, the two of them greet each other with enormous smiles.* JESSE *throws out his arms*) Muriel!

BEAT 1

Muriel: ¹(*smiles, cocks her head*) Jesse?

Jesse: It's not.

Muriel: ²It is. ³(*Pause*)

Jesse: Muriel, I can't believe it. Is it really you?

Muriel: It's me, Muriel.

Jesse: Well, come on in, for Pete's sakes, come on in.

BEAT 2

Muriel: [4] (*enters with a rush and crosses to the far side of the sofa*)[5] I can only stay for a few minutes.

Jesse: (*closes the door and follows her to below the near side of the sofa*) My God, it's good to see you. (*They stand and confront each other*)

Muriel: [6] I just dropped in to say hello. [7] I really can't stay.

Jesse: You sounded good on the phone, but you look even better.

Muriel: [8] Because I've got to get back to New Jersey. [9] I'm parked in a one hour zone. [10] Hello, Jesse. [11] I think I'm very nervous.

Jesse: Hey! Hello, Muriel.

Super objective: To win Jesse's adoration

Spine: To captivate

Major Obstacle: Sex (I'm married)

Main Action: To flirt

Main Objective: To win his affection

Scene Tag: The Initial Flirtation

Inner images for Muriel's initial entrance: Jesse is a visiting celebrity. I am a suburban housewife. I have not seen him since our high school romance days. I have never been inside the Plaza Hotel before.

Major substitution: John Kennedy for Jesse.

Initially walk through lobby to elevator to seventh floor, down hall (if someone sees me?). I don't belong here. Going to "Kennedy's" private suite is dangerous reputation-wise. Newsmen are always on the heels of famous people—looking for a flash story. Ted—Chappaquiddick. They could unearth all kinds of stories about my past. I live 1½ hours from here. JFK is an international celebrity. My family and friends are vulnerable for they don't even know I'm here. JFK doesn't live in NYC—special visit = more newsmen. I must get inside his apartment, although I don't know if he's alone within. He's been in NYC many times since we were together.

I was in the kitchen at 5:30 yesterday when Jesse called from New York. Children Elizabeth and John were watching TV; Larry was working. I never know whether Larry's coming home for dinner or not.

ACTION	OBJECTIVE	OBSTACLE	INNER IMAGE
BEAT 1			
1. to question	elicit his reason for calling me	he turns me on (main obstacle)	USC, short hair, glasses
2. to confirm it's me	elicit his reason for calling me		away long time and return home
3. to reconfirm	convince how well preserved I am	I'm married! (time, hotel hall, bedroom)	hair a mess, no sleep, shoes un-polished, outfit wrinkled, see apartment
BEAT 2			
4. to flirt: "same old me"	convince how well preserved I am		
5. to warn	expose his reason for calling		protect self
6. to convince of quick social visit	expose his mo-tive for ravish-ing me	time on meter	excuse exit, return to Daddy
7. to tease	expose his motive for ravishing me		my "dignity"
8. to disregard compliment	titillate to expose desire	gorgeous room	
9. to postpone affair	warn to act dignified	nerves	muscled = David, he's hot, demands of Jersey
10. to confront lover honestly	remind of past intimacy	his fame	meter by Bonwit's

ACTION	OBJECTIVE	OBSTACLE	INNER IMAGE
11. to define fear	nurture sympathy for erratic actions		G.N. restaurant

AH, WILDERNESS!, ACT 4, SCENE 2: RICHARD'S SCORE

[1] (RICHARD *starts to stroll around with exaggerated carelessness, turning his back on the path, hands in pockets,* [2] *whistling with insouciance "Waiting at the Church."*)

[3] (MURIEL MCCOMBER *enters from down the path, left front. She is fifteen, going on sixteen. She is a pretty girl with a plump, graceful little figure, fluffy, light-brown hair, big naive wondering dark eyes, a round dimpled face, a melting drawly voice. Just now she is in a great thrilled state of timid adventurousness.* [4] *She hesitates in the shadow at the foot of the path, waiting for* RICHARD *to see her,* [5] *but he resolutely goes on whistling with back turned, and she has to call him.*)

Muriel: Oh, Dick.

Richard: [6] (*turns around with an elaborate simulation of being disturbed in the midst of profound meditation.*) [7] Oh, hello. [8] Is it nine already? [9] Gosh, time passes—[10] when you're thinking.

Muriel: (*coming toward him as far as the edge of the shadow—disappointedly*) I thought you'd be waiting right here at the end of the path. I'll bet you'd forgotten I was even coming.

Richard: [11] (*strolling a little toward her but not too far—carelessly*) [12] No, I hadn't forgotten, [13] honest. [14] But I got to thinking about life.

Muriel: You might think of me for a change, after all the risks I've run to see you! (*hesitating timidly on the edge of the shadow*) Dick! You come here to me. I'm afraid to go out in that bright moonlight where anyone might see me.

Richard: (*coming to her—scornfully*) [15] Aw, there you go again—always scared of life!

Super Objective: To marry Muriel
Spine: To capture Muriel
Major Obstacle: Her resistance
Main Action: To punish

Main Objective: To torment with desire

Scene Tag: The Making-Up Scene

ACTION	OBJECTIVE	OBSTACLE	INNER IMAGE
1. to stalk	to hide rejection	broken heart	dear John letter
2. to whistle	to hide feelings	she's late	broken agreement
3. to sneak a look	to see if she loves me	darkness	softness of skin
4. to adore	to find a sign of her love	her treachery	Judy O
5. to peal music	to comfort self	her treachery	N. D. alone
6. to condescend	to belittle	her cruelty	
7. to dismiss	to rub it in	feeling of tragedy	dear John kiss
8. to disbelieve	to ignore her	her abandonment	
9. to discount	to distance	her sore feet	suicide of M. S.
10. to proclaim	to lessen her importance	passionate feeling	her letter
11. to play hard to get	to lessen her importance	her full figure	sand
12. to hesitate	to seize comfort	her coldness	Q. R. at pit
13. to reassure	to seize comfort	shadows	cast-off ice
14. to philosophize	to recover pride	her rejection	cast-off letter
15. to scorn	to excite adventure	her love for Dad	her father's hat

How do I set choices with my score?

Setting choices means finalizing the score for your performance. Your performance may still ripen emotionally, but essentially your plan for the role is solidified. Because a pause or an inappropriate movement can destroy momentum, eventually every actor needs to stick to what has been rehearsed and researched. In an improvisation, you're freely inventing as you go. But making your choices for a script spontaneous can result only from knowing what your form is—by keeping a score.

How does the score help me in performance?

Chance favors the prepared mind.

Louis Pasteur

The longer the run of the play, the more valuable an accurate score becomes. It protects you from losing your bearings onstage. Because of it, you will always be able to repeat your most brilliant performance. After opening night, you can continue to enrich your score. After they are in the run, many actors still work on their scores several hours a day—deepening choices, emotionally charging the body and voice.

To keep your score alive over a long period of time, keep working as your own coach. Most people will accept a certain level of quality from you. They don't really push you to the ultimate homework you can do. Are you training your body and voice? All that takes tremendous personal discipline. No one makes you write a score, create a background, do research, or experiment! It's not like being on an athletic team where the coach reprimands you if you don't train.

The score allows you to play free—to act with great expressiveness—because it supports you with an invisible framework. You contact your burning passion—the major objective in the scene—and then you play 100 percent to get it.

How can I use a checklist for the score?

After you have developed a certain ability to score, use this checklist to enrich your emotional life onstage. Follow this outline loosely, using it as a reference more than as a bible, and adjust it to your needs because it will vary somewhat with each actor and with each character.

■ CHECKLIST

What am I urgently doing and why?

A. Line Analysis
   1. What am I doing on each line and why? What do I want from my partner and what is stopping me? (What is the action, the objective, and the obstacle? For example, "I want to make him laugh in order to win his confidence; but he ignores me.")
   2. Who or what is my object of attention on what line? Where is my focus? (This can sometimes be the same throughout the play.) What inner image am I experiencing?
   3. What activity, bit of business, or gesture can I find that will support my action, clarify it, strengthen it?
   4. What adjustment must I take, if any, toward the line? (Consider to whom the line is being said, the place, the time, and circumstances surrounding it to determine how it should be said.)

B. Beat Analysis
   1. Follow outline for line analysis.
   2. A beat is a unit within a scene that has a beginning, a middle, and an end. Each beat is determined by finding each change within each scene, such as the entrance or exit of a character, a new objective or obstacle, that changes the subject under discussion.
   3. The analysis of the beat (action and objective) depends on the analysis of the lines within the beat. The actions of the lines, linked together, determine the action of the beat.
   4. What is the transitional line between beats? One beat does not necessarily stop suddenly and another begin, but often something or someone ties one to the other, such as the entrance of another person or a new circumstance.

C. Scene Analysis
   1. Follow outline for line analysis.
   2. In finding the scenes, use script scene designations to begin with.
   3. The analysis of the scene's action and objective depends on the analysis of the beats within that scene. The actions of beats, linked together, determine the action of the scene.
   4. Find the character traits you will try to blend with each of the important or emphasized elements (beats) in the play.

D. Act Analysis
   1. Follow outline for line analysis.
   2. The analysis of the act depends on the analysis of the scenes within that act. The actions of the scenes, linked together, determine the action of the act.
   3. By linking all these together you can determine the overall objective, or super objective, of your character in the play.
   4. Select the most important elements (usually beats) you will emphasize in performance. These are the ones most directly linked to your super objective in the play.

■ FINAL PROJECTS

1. *Score a Progressive Exercise.* This exercise relates to the previous ones in chapters 1–4, so you have the same partner.

   EXERCISE 5:   An empty courtroom. Two years have passed. You and your partner are intensely related. The exercise is scored in three beats.

   Beat 1 begins as you each play an opposing action, objective, obstacle, and inner image. Begin the scene in silence, with each of you engaged in a physical activity. Then one of you should begin the verbal conflict.

   Beat 2 begins when a second couple enters (possibly your partners from a previous exercise). Actions, objectives, obstacles, and inner images shift.

   Beat 3 occurs when still another couple enters, and a new conflict erupts. (Note: If the class is small, couples from the entire class can ultimately enter the conflict of the scene.) Hand in written background and score the elements of all three beats.

2. *Score a Scene.* Rehearse a scene from a play (see Appendix A). Determine the opposing objectives, your overall action, super objective, obstacle, and inner images. Ask yourself, "Is my interior monologue related to the same stream of consciousness as the character's? Am I journeying through

the same life experience?" Do a line-by-line score of the scene.

3. *Score an Article.* Choose an article from a magazine or newspaper. Score the article as a monologue, deciding who it is addressed to and noting line-by-line actions, objectives, obstacles, and inner images. Perform the monologue in class.

4. *Score Your Beats.* Rehearse a structured improvisation in which your objective and your partner's totally conflict. Each should pick a passionate opposing point of view that you can personally relate to. Each of you should choose an activity. Start with two minutes of silence that erupt into a verbal conflict. The scene should last five minutes and stop when one of you wins or calls a halt.

6
CHARACTER
Who am I?

**This chapter deals with character—the distinguishing features
of an individual. Who you are affects how you act.**

Unless you use your text to advantage you cannot act. Preliminary study
is seeking to learn the facts about your character. You have to go to your
author to get these. His words cannot mean anything unless you get his
meaning behind the words. Creating a character is like building a house.
You have to accumulate the material with which to build it.

Charles Jehlinger, founder of the American Academy of Dramatic Arts

■ WHAT IS CHARACTER?

Character is the distinguishing features of a person—looks,
feelings, and actions. It is the "how" of action. How we do
something depends on who we are. After we know what we are
doing onstage, we must discover how we do it. We must become the character.

What is becoming the character?

Becoming the character is developing the physical and psychological traits of the role. Each of you in life plays a character and
does things in a certain way. So linked are you to your own character that when you are out of sorts, you may be surprised when
others remark, "You're not yourself today." Observation helps
you identify distinctions necessary to becoming the character.

Sometimes in my classes, I will assign each actor to come to class like a fellow actor. The actor must wear the same clothes and act exactly like that other person. I then come to class like another teacher and behave totally differently—soft spoken, cautious, slow moving. The actors keep asking me whether I'm mad or sick. The point is that in order to play someone else, you must adjust how you behave.

When you look at the character you're to play you must ask yourself, "Who am I?" Using the "I" will help you identify with the character. Your aim is to give yourself a new background, to embrace all the elements of the new you. You begin developing the new you through observation and reflection. You observe the inner and outer worlds of others, attempting to grow into the part.

■ OBSERVATION

Genius is the talent for seeing things straight . . . without any bend or break or aberration of sight, without any warping of vision.

Maude Adams, American actress, 1872–1953

What is observation?

Observation is the acting technique of being aware of yourself and others offstage. Zoom in on details of dress and physical behavior. Look around you and try to notice someone with an interesting body and voice, or someone behaving in a special way. Study that person's gestures, body movements, tones of voice, posture, and clothes, and imagine yourself becoming that person.

What is an observation exercise?

An observation exercise is one in which you notice and record another's behavior and restage it in class.

Begin by observing the physical traits. As you move into the creation of a character's thoughts and feelings, you will identify and copy the more subtle actions of the soul.

1. *The Stranger.* Observe a stranger doing some activity such as eating or shopping. Record only the physical actions and re-create them in class. Afterward, tell the class the thoughts you suspect may have prompted these physical actions. Imitate the stranger exactly. Try to experience how different gestures and rhythms feel.

2. *My Style.* Stand opposite a partner. Walk toward the partner reciting your name and vital statistics, then have him/her do the same. What did each of you notice about how the other person moved and spoke? Now imitate that.

3. *Professional Procedure.* Observe one of the following groups of people. Write down and re-create the actions of a person in one group. Stage the sequence.

   a. three waiters or waitresses serving
   b. three freshmen studying
   c. three beauticians combing hair
   d. three teachers lecturing
   e. three janitors cleaning

4. *Character Description.* Take notes, then describe in detail your father, mother, or best friend. Use precise words: She speaks in measured tones; has long, red, perfectly manicured nails; prefers black or navy accessories; and so forth.

■ CHARACTER ANALYSIS

What is a character analysis?

Character analysis is evaluating the play for background, the sum of your character's experiences, training, or education. In the next part of this chapter you will look at how you apply an understanding of the play to developing your role. First and foremost, your character must fit into and advance the play. Reread the script to discover tidbits of information.

The character must not change the play's overall direction and meaning. The character must work for the play. Some characters are aggressive, self-centered, blindly ambitious, or savage, with few redeeming features. The actor must expose the breadth of negative traits that work for the play.

The audience can recognize those traits. Watching them performed, the audience obtains greater self-knowledge, a relief, or catharsis. You need to dig for the truth, whether or not you personally like the traits that are unearthed.

How do I study a script for character?

Look for facts about your character. Start by simply trying to understand the language. As the lines become clearer, search for clues to your character. Ask yourself, "What is my character's function in the play? When and why do I enter a scene? What do I and others say about my character?"

You must discern from deep study of the play facts about your family, rearing, education, friends, well-being, talent, and hobbies. Look for your character's main desires, what thoughts your character leans upon, your subconscious needs.

In studying the character, you may need to face certain traits you don't like about yourself. Perhaps your character is healthier, in better shape, more educated than you. These are areas you will need to work on to grow into the character.

■ PHYSICAL TRAITS

What physical traits should I look for?

You begin any character analysis with a study of physical traits. These are the easiest to grasp and will lead to an understanding of your character's psychological traits. The physical is the most obvious level of characterization because it reveals external traits: sex, age, size, color, health, fitness, vocal quality, physical quality (fast or slow). Sixty percent of what you reveal to the audience about your character is how you comb your hair, how you gesture, how you dress.

Think about yourself right now. Are you tall, short, shapely, a bit overweight? Are your eyes blue, is your hair brown, is that your natural color? How old are you? Do you look your age? Would you describe yourself as attractive—do others see you as such? Are your clothes stylish? Are you dressed for class or for work? Are you healthy? Is your lifestyle active or sedentary?

Imagine your character's physical life. Were you a healthy child? Are you athletic? Were you in the service? Do you like the outdoors? What is your work background?

Note the physical differences between the two brothers Eugene O'Neill describes in *Long Day's Journey into Night*, act 1, scene 1. These facts are taken directly from character descriptions in the play.

LONG DAY'S JOURNEY: CHARACTER DESCRIPTIONS

JAMIE	EDMUND
Physique	
Broad-shouldered, deep-chested physique; is an inch taller than his father and weighs less, but appears shorter and stouter because he lacks bearing and graceful carriage	Looks taller than Jamie; thin and wiry; more like his mother
Coloring	
Fair skin is sunburned a reddish, freckled tan	Sunburned a deep brown, but with a parched sallowness
Age	
Thirty-three	Twenty-three
Face	
Good-looking, despite marks of dissipation; never been handsome; resembles father; fine brown eyes; hair	*Big, dark eyes* are the dominant feature in his long Irish face; hypersensitiveness; high forehead; dark brown

is thinning, and already there is an indication of a bald spot; aquiline without sneering	hair, sun-bleached to red at the ends, brushed straight back; nose like his father's

Hands

Sunburned, a reddish, freckled tan	*Exceptionally long fingers;* nervous

Health

Lacks vitality; signs of premature disintegration are on him	Nervous sensibility; in bad health and thinner than he should be, with feverish eyes and sunken cheeks

Clothes

Dressed in an *old sack suit;* wears collar and tie	Dressed in a *shirt, collar,* and a tie; no coat, old flannel trousers, brown sneaker

To play Jamie, or any role, you must decide how each physical trait affects your action. For example, Jamie is described as lacking vitality. Imagine what causes this. Jamie the character is based on O'Neill's brother. Several symptoms could cause Jamie's lack of vitality. But as you read the play you discover that alcoholism is the cause.

Identify real problems to deal with onstage. Is Jamie protecting his gruff voice already scratched from too much shouting in bars? Does he lumber along awkwardly because he's a bit high? Practice various choices. With your director's help, pick the interpretation that works best for you.

Does my character have a handicap?

Some characters operate with a permanent disability. If your character has a handicap, you will need to spend time researching and making it real for yourself. If you are the blind Helen Keller, practice the scene (under careful supervision) blindfolded. Experiment at home with getting dressed or eating when blindfolded. If you are lame like Laura, wrap part of your leg in a bandage. Use a stone in the bandage for a soreness, a real metal brace for polio, and so on. Test possible physical ailments and adjustments.

Some conditions, such as an epileptic seizure or drunkenness, may be temporary. Identify that sensation and what it does to the body. Let that lead you to the adjustment to overcome it. For drunkenness, a thick tongue (sensation) makes you enunciate (adjustment). Instead of simply being "drunk," determine the specific site of the discomfort (tongue won't move, so you must overarticulate). Rehearse the scene first normally, then add the adjustments.

What is my character's profession?

The profession of your character may affect how you act. Although both in their sixties, James Tyrone (the actor) and Willy Loman (the salesman) have been handicapped by different professions. James Tyrone seems taller because of his theatrical bearing. His voice is remarkably fine, resonant, and flexible. His speech, movement, and gestures reveal a studied acting technique. Willy is dressed quietly, slouches, and talks to himself. He heaves a sigh and flinches his sore palms, the effect of years of lugging heavy sales cases.

Does my character act like an animal?

You can use traits of animals and objects to expand your characterizations. Is your character like an animal, machine, or object? Do you lumber like an old stag? Dart about like a mouse? The traits of animals are graphic and communicate immediately with an audience. Think of how expressive the movement of a monkey, crane, or tiger can be. Going to the zoo can stimulate your imagination. Watch a hippopotamus snort, a monkey fidget, a bat flutter, an elephant swagger. Listen to a pig and a seal; they squeal differently. Observe how an animal defends itself: A parrot shrieks, a peacock fans its tail, a lizard hides.

Some writers cite animals for certain characters, as in the films *Beauty and the Beast* and *Wolfman* and the plays *The Lion in Winter*, *The Elephant Man*, and *Cat on a Hot Tin Roof* (the lead, Maggie, even refers to herself as a cat). Through *observation*, become aware of how expressive animals can be.

Does my character act like a machine?

Close your eyes and listen to the rhythmic sounds of machines around you (humming clothes dryer, clicking computer, screaming doorbell, grinding alarm clock, straining car, shrieking phone). What if you clicked your teeth like a metronome or groaned like an industrial vacuum? The traits of machines can add an exciting dimension to your role. In some roles, mechanical traits predominate: Robocop, C3PO, the Tin Man.

How should I rehearse physical traits?

Attend rehearsals dressed hat to shoes in character. If you are practicing in tennis shoes, whereas your character would really be wearing spike heels, you're wasting your time. Wearing the appropriate clothes helps you experience the necessary changes in posture, breathing, and speech from the beginning.

The best costumes lead to a revelation of character. For example, if your character is a glutton, which coat do you pick? How about practicing with a coat that's too tight? Or a coat with a seam split out?

Refer to your character as "I" rather than as "he" or "she." Say "I am doing this," not "He is doing this." By uniting yourself with your character, you begin imagining his actions.

EXERCISES

1. *Physical Trait.* Play the action "to pack a suitcase," "to fix breakfast," or "to rearrange the room." Use one of the following handicaps: crippled, obese, blind, surgery patient, arthritic, pregnant.

2. *Imaginary Garment.* Wear an article of clothing (such as high heels, back brace, straw hat) that restricts your behavior. Do a task. Then do the same task not wearing the garment but using it as an imaginary influence.

3. *Different Uniforms.* Create an improvisation in which you and a partner imitate two waiters. Find the differences between the two. Now switch roles.

4. *Blindman's Bluff.* Play blindman's bluff (also called Marco Polo). Blindfold and spin around one member of the class. Classmates hide around the room as he counts to fifteen. The blind person must touch and identify someone to win.

5. *Physical Condition.* Play the action of "to apply makeup" or "to shave" with the physical condition of being drunk, sleepy, or nauseated.

6. *Character Tasks.* Demonstrate the following tasks as two different characters: (a) to enter a room; (b) to stand on a chair; (c) to remove your shoes; (d) to kneel; (e) to leave the room. Do not change the order of the tasks.

7. *Observing Body Positions.* Demonstrate ten ways to do one of the following:
   a. sit in a chair
   b. lounge on the floor
   c. lean by a door

■ PSYCHOLOGICAL TRAITS

What are psychological traits?

Psychological traits are the distinguishing qualities of your character. Psychological traits reveal a character's habitual motivations, likes, and dislikes—the emotional and intellectual aspects of character that inspire action. Education, social background, religion, and type of work are significant here. Childhood environment, class background, and work experiences all affect your thought. Your character's dominant attitude (positive/negative), beliefs, and moral and social class all influence thought and psychological traits. Psychological traits can be strengthened by knowing your character's inner motive forces, feelings, mind, will.

How do inner motive forces work?

The first, and most important master (is) *feeling* . . . unfortunately it is not tractable. . . . Since you cannot begin your work unless your feelings happen to function of their own accord, it is necessary for you to have recourse to some other master. . . . Who is it? The second master is the *mind*. . . . Your mind can be a motive power in . . . your creative process. Is there a third? . . . If longings could put your creative apparatus to work and direct it spiritually . . . we have found our third master—*will*. Consequently we have three impelling movers in our psychic life. Since these three forces form a triumvirate, inextricably bound up together, what you say of the one necessarily concerns the other two. . . . This combined power is of utmost importance to us actors and we should be gravely mistaken not to use it for our practical ends. . . . Actors whose feelings over-balance their intellects will, naturally, in playing Romeo or Othello, emphasize the emotional side. Actors in whom the will is the most powerful attribute will play Macbeth or Brand and underscore ambition or fanaticism. The third type will unconsciously stress, more than is necessary, the intellectual shadings of a part like Hamlet or Nathan the Wise.

It is however necessary not to allow any one of these three elements to crush out either of the others and thereby upset the balance and necessary harmony. Our art recognizes all three types and in their creative work all three forces play leading parts in shaping psychological action. (*Stanislavski Handbook*, pp. 82–83)

Why are psychological traits challenging?

Psychological traits are every bit as important as physical traits but are less tangible. In Tennessee Williams's *Cat on a Hot Tin Roof* Brick has a broken leg; he wears a cast and uses a crutch. His physical handicap is obvious to the audience. Brick is depressed, tormented, but sexually appealing. What kind of choices can Brick make to communicate these feelings to the audience?

What do you do when you feel depressed? Do you withdraw, shut the door to your room, and crawl into bed? Do you overeat? Do you snap at people who try to befriend you? Do you neglect yourself physically—not combing your hair, not tying your shoes?

Onstage you must convey your depression to your audience immediately and dramatically. You may decide to investigate what you have to subtract from and add to your action to expose and sustain your depression as Brick.

How should I rehearse psychological traits?

Test instinctive choices. What is your immediate response to impersonating a snob? Think of snobs you have known. What did they do? Keep their distance? Wait for people to approach them? Speak in a measured tone? Hold their head high? Dress better than everyone else? Smirk at others' failures? Try those choices and keep the ones that work for you in the scene.

Watch children at play. When you see kids on a playground, and their imaginations are racing, if one says, "Okay, I'll be the fairy princess, and you be the wicked witch," the other doesn't respond, "Give me ten minutes to get in touch with my wicked witch." She responds automatically from a sense of truth, and so should you.

How do impulses relate to my character?

Discovering your character's impulses is the root of all truthful interpretations. You must learn to connect with the appropriate reactions for the character. The more you can arouse the necessary feelings in your heart and body, the more you can channel your spirit into the role. A big part of acting is creating the environment for the strongest impulse-based reaction. What is your character sensing at this moment? Do you feel confused, uplifted? How is that emotion located in your body? What are you going to do because of that impulse? We live in a highly sophisticated technological society. Yet, in art, it is often the primitive, intuitive reaction that provokes interest.

A vital part of actor training is to nurture through spontaneous exercises the identification and personal involvement required in creating a role. You must discover and (most important of all) learn to trust impulses as the authentic raw material of acting.

How can playing games help me develop my impulses?

Contact is arguably the trigger for impulses. Develop the habit of really connecting with another actor, with another part of yourself, with the audience. Playing games can help you make contact with others and get in touch with your impulses. In every game, as in every sequence, you act spontaneously, and you play to win. Play games to loosen yourself up and relax: number games, word games, face-feels, where everybody tries to recognize one another. Provoke a gale of laughter from a partner.

Play games and enact fairy tales that fire you to behave preposterously for a goal. Onstage, you move and speak almost twice as much as in life. Games prepare you for this intensified activity by sharpening your instincts. Fairy tales emphasize the glamour of largeness and offer condensed images that open Pandora's box.

You can invent as many types of improvisations as there are games. Your improvisations can have one or numerous guidelines. You can also use improvisations as a spot-check of principles studied in class. There are many types of brief extemporaneous exercises that you can do alone or in groups to heighten your technique. When doing them, employ real objects to trick your impulses into full involvement.

EXERCISES

1. *Fairy Tale.* Act out your favorite fairy tale.

2. *Total War.* The object of this improvisation is never to stop making verbal sounds or talking. Two people go onstage and verbally attack each other. First option: two roommates. One condemns the other for wrecking the car; one for destroying a best outfit. Second option: a newly married

couple. She attacks him for losing interest. He attacks her for flirting with his best friend.

3. *Giant Exercise.* Think and act like a giant, like somebody big. Say your name as loudly as you can to startle your partner.

4. *Mirror Exercise.* In pairs, stand opposite each other. Choose a leader to perform a physical movement and a follower to simultaneously mirror the action. Send a classmate out of the room, and rearrange the leaders in each pair. Objective: to prevent your classmate from identifying the leaders.

5. *Calling Qualities.* Play the action "to straighten the room." Adjust your interpretation as your teacher calls out, "You are lazy, shrewish, depressed, angry," and so on.

6. *Emphasizing Traits.* Interpret a scene two ways by emphasizing different personality traits. Possible adjectives to implement include *lazy, outgoing, hyper, shy, determined, pensive, violent.*

7. *The Bouncing Ball.* Bounce a ball in five different ways: like a sad, ecstatic, sluggish, withdrawn, and irritable person. Notice how easy it is to move from one trait to the next.

8. *Character Action.* List actions you would undertake when finding yourself in a doctor's office, a graveyard, or an empty park. Then list actions a famous person might undertake. Stage the action first performed your way, then the way of the celebrity.

9. *Psychological Trait.* Play a short sequence in which you perform one action. Use a trait of your offstage behavior, such as being disorganized, scatterbrained, distant, sexy, and so on throughout the scene.

10. *Character Analysis.* Analyze a character in a scene for physical and psychological traits. Use a play from Appendix A or B or one your teacher suggests. Optional: Stage a short sequence.

11. *Character Improvisation.* Pick one of your favorite characters in a play. Try to get into the skin of the character by practicing one or more of the following improvisations as your character. Stage one of the improvisations for class.

getting dressed	coming home from work
eating breakfast	talking on the phone to
reading the mail	a lover
handling problems at work	going to bed

■ CHECKLIST

This checklist should help you explore exciting details about your character. Answering these questions should encourage a vigorous approach to characterization.

1. How does my character develop the play?

2. What physical traits affect the way I speak and move?

3. What are my distinctive psychological traits?

■ WHAT IS A HISTORY?

A history is a written record of events and feelings in a character's life. It includes all the factors affecting your stage action. In real life, you are the consequences of all history preceding this moment. And you will be the consequences of all history following this moment. Your history is so significant that many cultures identify individuals by their forefathers, parents, neighborhood, and address. You can never ignore, nor make too much of, your character's history. Understanding the past leads to specific action in the here and now of the performance.

Good actors write down their character's history. They invent emotional experiences that prompt a flood of memories, thoughts, and sensations. These experiences create a stream of consciousness for them onstage and shape the course of their actions. Through conscious means, they are expanding their imagination to embrace the unconscious: the spirit of their character.

Many actors keep a daily journal of observations about their character's background, which they refer to when writing the history. Recording pertinent details helps them integrate their role with real-life observation.

A word of advice: Whenever doing a history, always consult your director. You want to compose a scenario that works with his or her vision of the play. A production with all of the actors writing histories supporting that vision can possess an unusual focus.

How does the past shape the present?

Twentieth-century psychology has illuminated our understanding of the past's influences on the present. Remember two important principles: (1) The brain functions as a high-fidelity tape, recording the feelings associated with past experiences. (2) Recorded experiences and the feelings associated with them are available for replay today in their original vivid form and largely determine the nature of today's transactions. The breakthrough discovery is that an event and the feeling produced by it are inextricably locked together in the brain. One cannot be evoked without the other. We record not only past events in detail but also the feelings—sensations, emotions, sensitivities, tolerances, excitabilities—associated with them. The following report by the pioneering psychologist Carl Jung in *Man and His Symbols* illustrates the way present stimulations evoke past feelings:

> A forty-year-old female patient reported she was walking down the street one morning and, as she passed a music store, she heard a strain of music that produced an overwhelming melancholy. She felt herself in the grip of a sadness she could not understand, the intensity of which was almost unbearable. Nothing in her conscious thought could explain this. Later in the week she phoned me to tell me that, as she continued to hum the song

over and over, she suddenly had a flash of recollection in which she saw her mother sitting at the piano and heard her playing this song. The mother had died when the patient was five years old. I asked her if the recall of this early memory had relieved her depression. She said it had changed the nature of her feelings; there was still a melancholy feeling in recalling the death of her mother, but it was not the initial overwhelming despair she had felt at first. It would seem she was now consciously remembering a feeling which initially was the reliving of a feeling. In the second instance, she remembered how it was to feel that way; but in the first instance, the feeling was precisely the same feeling which was recorded when her mother died. She was at that moment five years old.

How does the history influence my stage actions?

Imagine yourself making a serious decision with no sense of your past, and you will experience how vapid a performance is without a history. So close are you to your own history that, like your shadow, you take it for granted. You speak, think, act, dream from your memories.

The history affects each action. If you feel melancholic, you might retreat to your room, call a friend, or aggravate a neighbor, depending on your history—what kind of person you are. A strong history of your character that is grounded in your own experiences and fantasies will stimulate you to choose actions appropriate to the character.

What is the emotional value of the history?

The history's value lies in how it weights your stage actions. In writing the history, you are finding feelings to fill moments onstage. Evoked recollection is not the exact photographic or phonographic reproduction of past scenes or events, but rather a reproduction of sensation: of what you saw, heard, felt, and understood. These palpable experiences can be both recalled and relived. I not only remember how I felt, but also I feel the same way now. Loading all you say onstage with your thoughts, feelings, and sensations from the past generates convincing action.

A history prepares the way for the climax, the "unconscious explosion" that will erupt onstage. For instance, in your character's day-to-day life your first priority could be to act like a loving wife. But your history (your parents' oppressive insistence on obedience and perfection, for example) may ripen you for the terrifying action of seducing your husband's best friend.

In writing the history for such a character (a character present in Harold Pinter's play *Betrayal*), you might create the mind-set of a "good wife" who is keenly aware of daily duties but blind to the dangerous tedium in her marriage.

■ WHAT IS A LIFE SCRIPT?

Some psychoanalysts, such as Eric Berne, view a history as your life script, which determines your outlook. Are you "waiting for Santa Claus" or "waiting for rigor mortis"? A history reflects a character's expectations—often unmet by the scene.

Writing your character's history should help you uncover the early decisions your character made unconsciously as to how life should be lived. Psychoanalyst L. S. Kubie wrote in a 1958 article in the *Journal of Mental Science:*

> Early in life, a central emotional position is frequently established which becomes the affective position to which that individual will tend to return automatically for the rest of his days. This in turn may constitute either the major safeguard or the major vulnerability of his life. . . . Whenever the central emotional position is painful . . . the individual may spend his whole life defending himself against it, again using conscious, preconscious, and unconscious devices whose aim it is to avoid this pain-filled central position. Your life script, formed in early childhood, may have gone through various "rewrites" as you grew up, with the plot and imagined ending remaining essentially unchanged.

How does my life script dictate my actions?

Your character acts not according to what things are really like, but rather according to his life script, which gives rise to mental images of what he perceives things to be. In *A Layman's Guide to Psychiatry and Psychoanalysis*, Eric Berne claims that "everyone has images of himself, the world, and others and behaves as though those images, rather than the objects they represent are the 'truth.'"

Your life script—how you see the world—creates the action. If you are waiting for Santa Claus, and your action is to get dressed, you might hum, dance into your stockings, put on bright clothes. If you are waiting for rigor mortis, you could slam off the alarm clock, curse, break your nail as you zip up your drab pants. Your outlook, which is formed by your experiences, actually determines what you do and how you do it. You are so allied to your own life script that you act spontaneously from it. You do certain things because of it. Wed yourself to your character's history, and you will choose specific actions appropriate to the character.

Berne observed, "What is called 'adaptability' depends on your ability to change images in your life script to correspond to a new reality. Most people can change some images but not others." Many characters cling to certain pictures and sensations that they refuse to discard.

■ DISCOVERING THE HISTORY

Why is my character's childhood important?

The "good old times"—all times when old are good—are gone.

Lord Byron

The mental and moral qualities of an individual are shaped by childhood, the most impressionable stage. Each human being is largely the product of her earliest experiences. Your capacity to govern your destiny is limited, to a much greater degree than you are ever conscious of, by patterns laid down sometimes even *before* birth.

Ask the following questions about your character: What were your parents' attitudes toward having children? Did they really want you? Why? Did one parent wish for a boy and the other a girl? Were they disappointed? How healthy were they physically? How stable emotionally? How sound is your genetic inheritance? How ideal were the environmental conditions in your mother's womb? What were the obstetrical circumstances of your birth?

Which childhood events may account for some of your behavior now? How do you feel about where you come from, what your upbringing was like, what your parents were like? What people did you know as an adolescent? Who influenced you to become the person you are now?

EXERCISES

1. *Yearly Diary.* Remember a significant emotional experience for each year of your own life, starting at your present age and moving backward. Do this daily between practice sessions. Keep a journal and fill in events for each year as a resource for your roles.

2. *Treasured Object.* Bring in a treasured object from a historical period, such as a doll from turn-of-the-century Britain, a pilot's helmet from World War II, a fan from the 1950s. Use your affection for the object to tell us something about a character in a particular play.

3. *Life Scripts.* Create two different, but explosive, life scripts for a character in the waiting room of a hospital. Based on these, stage two different interpretations of the action "to stall."

■ WRITING THE BIOGRAPHY

How do I write a history?

The actors in most professional training programs do two kinds
of biographies—a subjective and an objective one. A subjective biography is what the character knows. An objective biography is what the actor knows. I prefer the subjective biography because in writing it, you are submerging yourself in the
thoughts, feelings, and sensations of the character.

As you develop your character's history, use rehearsals to invent more facts. Obviously, the way the actress playing your
wife touches you should suggest what the marriage is like because the two of you are working on that story. The way your
brother and you argue should suggest your character's childhood. Acting is behaving as if the situation is real. Rehearsals
with your fellow actors should suggest your common history.

Why do actors who add nothing to the lines bore us? Because
the lines are lifeless. What you invent gives the role vitality.

How do I use my own history?

To find a history that wakes up your inner self, that makes you
very aware of each moment onstage, you must bring your own
personal past into the character's present. Massage your mind
with memories so that your interpretation of the events automatically suits the character. The more specific images you recall that are suited to the character, the more details and nuances of feeling will emerge in your performance. If you can
find nothing in common with your character, you may have to
expand on a few general experiences and use your memories of
films, books, and other people's lives. By the age of eighteen, we
all have experienced love, jealousy, rejection, ecstasy, loss, dis-
appointment, fear, anger—and all characters, no matter how
much they differ from you, experience some of these emotions
as well. If you enter the stage tuned into your own particular
emotional life, you will create a believable character and truth-

ful action. (See chapter 4, "Inner Images," for further discussion of this concept.)

It's one thing to tap experiences in ourselves and another thing to "live" a specific sequence of thoughts, feelings, and sensations throughout two hours. Although you should never risk a dangerous choice that might throw you out of control, to re-create the edges of human experience you will have to explore your own memories. You will bring the reality—raw and bold—of who you are to a role.

In our culture, people come to the theater *because* their lives are so *safe*. Besides entertainment, they come to the theater to learn about themselves and society. You, the actors, extend their vision by what you dare to reveal.

■ CHECKLIST

1. What are my character's age, weight, height, speech characteristics, walking/sitting/standing patterns, mannerisms or peculiarities, nationality, health, and level of vitality?

2. How does my character's past affect my present actions onstage?

3. What is my character's life script? How does it shape my point of view onstage?

■ FINAL PROJECTS

1. *Progressive Exercises.* Throughout the next few chapters, you will do a second series of related progressive exercises. Each shows you how the background element of that chapter interrelates with your entire performance. Each exercise strengthens a new area of your knowledge. Rehearse each sequence at least three times with your partner.

EXERCISE 1: An empty campus or park. Pick a partner. You are strangers with opposing traits. For example, one of you is neat, and one is sloppy, or one is nervous, one relaxed. Your character traits affect all you do throughout the scene. Begin the exercise with each of you performing one action in silence, then one of you begins a conflict between you. Beginning with silence allows the action to come from the heart, not the words.

EXERCISE 2: This exercise builds on Progressive Exercise 3 for character (the empty park). Interrelate an understanding of history with your action as the character. An empty apartment. Use the same partner from Progressive Exercise 1. You are the same character, but two years have now passed, and you have developed an intense relationship. An intense relationship means you have shared many important experiences. Develop a detailed biography for yourself. Together work out a common history and create an empty apartment that is bristling with memories for you both. Rehearse this exercise at least three times with your partner. Begin the sequence with two minutes of silence, with each of you performing a physical task in the place. Then a conflict erupts between you. Don't let the term "empty apartment" stifle your creativity. Bring in objects loaded with meaning to support your task and conflict.

2. *Autobiography.* Write a history for a role that you have recently played or want to play. Create this history from the point of view of the character at a given age (growing up, before marriage, working).

   Optional: *Operative Word.* Based on your history, decide which words are the operative or most important ones in a scene. In rehearsal, touch your partner on those particular words. Stage the sequence for class.

3. *Nightmare.* Write a history for a nightmare you have had, then stage it. Write from your point of view as a helpless adolescent. You are driven into and must submit to overwhelm-

ing circumstances. Relax as you pursue a series of extreme actions. Rehearse using objects from your own past. Stage a sequence from the nightmare.

4. *An Interview.* Set up a radio or television interview conducted by one character with another in which the interviewee is asked biological questions.

5. *Collage.* Create a collage that could graphically illustrate a character's inner life. Imagine in the collage what kind of beverage, odor, flower, house, and season that your character could be.

7

SETTING
Where am I?

This chapter deals with establishing the scene's time and place, which allows you to respond sensitively to your action.

The weight of this sad time we must obey; Speak what we feel, not what we ought to say. The oldest hath borne most: we that are young Shall never see so much, nor live so long.

Shakespeare, *King Lear,* act 5, scene 3

■ WHAT IS THE SETTING?

Why do I need to study setting?

Setting is the time and place of a scene. When you walk onto a stage, you are always walking into a specific setting. In real life, you never forget the time and place. Onstage, in a make-believe setting, you need to keep contact with that vacant park at dusk, that waiting room at dawn, or that stifling noonday apartment. A vivid setting is central to today's stage productions and films. Some directors, like Joseph Chaikin, preconceive no spatial characteristics but work with designers throughout rehearsals to develop the environment with the performances.

■ THE TIME

What is time?

Stage time is a special period in which your character's action occurs. When it is influences what you do. Just as in real life, time onstage stimulates action. When you move onstage, you are doing so for a timely reason. You are getting a cup of morning coffee, answering the door for the noon mail, waiting for a seven o'clock date. So at 8 A.M., June 1, 1991, you might be getting dressed for work in a linen suit or watching the TV news, whereas at 6 P.M., November 1, 1943, you could be raking leaves, reading news about the war, or listening to the radio. Your words come forth from a context of time.

How many of us would not dress and deal with a brisk Sunday morning in a different way than with a sticky, humid Monday at dawn?

But how do you create a Sunday morning quality? You ask yourself what you would wear and do on a Sunday morning. For example, you might wear a kimono, sip coffee, and loll around the patio table with a newspaper. On a Monday at dawn, you might slip into a business suit and eat breakfast on the run as you pack your briefcase. Most plays sketch out the time, and you the actor must complete the details.

How do I rehearse for time?

As you practice, keep examining the question, "What would I be wearing and doing at this time?" Evaluate your costume. Are you pulling on a heavy winter coat, muffler, and cap, or are you lounging in your silk pajamas? Ask yourself, "What rituals—answering phone calls, responding to mail, getting my hair done—are particular to this special day, this Monday as opposed to this Saturday?" For example, if your scene is set on a noisy Friday in a dorm room, start running through activities like answering the phone, leaving messages for your roommate, sorting out clothes to wear Friday night. Conversely, the activities for a teacher then might include packing up books, erasing the blackboard, storing charts.

Imagine what details each of your senses is responding to while doing the activity. For instance, if you are getting dressed at 6 A.M., you might hear the ignition of a neighbor's car, smell bread from a nearby bakery, see the sunlight filter through the blinds.

How do I create a different era?

Looking like a person in a different era also depends on your clothing and behavior. You must understand the era to choose convincing actions. Watch films, listen to music, read historical novels to experience an earlier time. For example, how might you act after an evening banquet in the first century A.D.? What would you be wearing then at midnight? Imagine yourself cast as the young Syrian in *Salome* by Oscar Wilde. How would you respond to a milieu of soldiers, pages, slaves, Jews, and Nazarenes at the Palace of Herod? What would a Syrian of that era be doing—gossiping about the palace, watching veiled dancers, drinking at the cistern, socializing at banquets?

The boldfaced words in the opening scene from *Salome* show information about time to be evaluated.

SALOME: TIME CLUES

*A great terrace in the Palace of Herod, set above the **banqueting hall**. Some **soldiers are leaning over the balcony**. To the right there is a gigantic staircase, to the left, at the back, an old cistern surrounded by a wall of green bronze. **Moonlight.***

The Young Syrian:	How beautiful is the Princess Salome tonight!
The Page of Herodias:	Look at the moon! How strange the moon seems! She is like a woman rising from a tomb. She is like a dead woman. You would fancy she was looking for dead things.

The Young Syrian:	She has a strange look. She is like a little princess who wears a yellow veil, and whose feet are of silver. She is like a princess who has little white doves for feet. **You would fancy she [the moon] was dancing.**
The Page of Herodias:	She is like a woman who is dead. She moves very slowly. **(Noise in the banqueting hall)**
First Soldier:	**What an uproar! Who are those wild beasts howling?**
Second Soldier:	The Jews. They are always like that. **They are disputing about their religion.**

Actor's notes: *It appears to be late at night after a wild banquet. The soldiers are supporting themselves on the balcony. Maybe they are tired from overeating? Could they be drunk? Why is the moon so peculiar? Does it portend evil, unnatural disturbances ahead? Perhaps the Jews are drunk and are disputing about religion into the wee hours. You must do some research into the moon and into the first century to fully evaluate the clues of the text.*

What should I emphasize in creating an era?

Onstage, you should emphasize the physical action of your character. In particular, you might explore the physical activities of a different time. A few select physical details can capture the reality of another period. Note the tasks an actor has jotted down for Richard in O'Neill's *Ah, Wilderness!*, set in a Connecticut beach town in 1906. The underlined activities are ones actually performed in the play.

AH, WILDERNESS!: RICHARD'S NOTES

Clothing:	slacks, long-sleeve shirt, black leather oxfords, straw hat
Activities:	
Indoors:	dominoes, cards (war, fish, old maid, solitaire, poker, wishing aces), <u>poetry books</u>, rubber ball, <u>letter writing</u> with an old-

	fashioned pen and inkwell, tic-tac-toe, checkers, dice, cross-word puzzles, diary writing, <u>piano</u>.
Outdoors:	tennis, volleyball, biking, pebble throwing, swimming, fishing, <u>throwing a straw hat</u>, swinging from a tree, folding newspaper boats, tracing names with a stick, flying a kite, playing bad-minton, "light my candle," hold fast all I give you.
Beach:	What could I do while waiting on the shore? Feel the murky water, throw second-rate pebbles, shake my unkempt hair in the breeze, trace names with a flimsy stick, search for whitened shells, dump sand from my itchy shoes, wade in the glowing water?

How does knowing the period allow me to think like my character?

By experiencing certain activities, you begin to think like your character. For example, if you're playing Richard in *Ah, Wilderness!* you might read books on Victorian manners and wonder why a teenager would follow these rules. Is Richard ignoring these rules? Why does he go to so much trouble to meet his girlfriend Muriel secretly on the beach? You might imagine Richard's family dinner table. What was the family like back then? How many children lived to their adolescence? What were his siblings like? Their health? Their values? You might study why parents behaved so rigidly at the table.

You could think about Muriel. Is her father an old dragon? Yes, except he's about forty, forty-five maybe, at the oldest. He knows that when unmarried girls get pregnant, they lose all their worth. You might ask yourself, "Where's Muriel's mother? Why are the women not controlling these youngsters?" Well, women weren't voting, driving cars, or even working back then. Note that Lily, the maiden aunt, still helps with the dinner and lives with Richard's family.

Then you might wonder why Richard's mother likes to sew and complain. She says things like: "If you don't stop talking Fourth of July—! To hear you go on, you'd think that was an excuse for anything from murder to picking pockets!" (act 3, scene 2).

You will find out that these Victorian parents are clinging by their fingernails to a very formal, cautious lifestyle, but the Goths are at the gate, so that's why they're so uptight. When your way of life is threatened, you either change or you clamp down and do it better. Suddenly, you might see behind the scenes where Richard slips away for the night, a bored teenager baffled by his parents' rules.

How do I rehearse another era?

To rehearse another era, test out your character's clothing and physical behavior. For example, the way Richard in *Ah, Wilderness!* moves is not something that you imagine. It's you on the beach with this damp straw hat, these conservative slacks, and these turn-of-the-century shoes and socks. You must duplicate what happened back then, obviously, with a contemporary sensibility. If you want to look carefree, like Richard, begin practicing with his shoes and clothing.

Knowing how people dressed and behaved in a certain period will help you choose specific actions. For example, leaving the Belle Reve plantation in the 1950s in *Streetcar*, Blanche is likely to act out of place in Stanley Kowalski's tiny slum apartment on the fringes of the French Quarter. Note Williams's poignant character descriptions, suggesting a clash in activities of the two main characters. Observe the details of the period: the paper-wrapped package from the local butcher, the bowling jacket (a big item in the 1950s), and the white gloves and hat worn by upper-class women when going anywhere in that decade.

STANLEY *is about twenty-eight or thirty years old, roughly dressed in blue denim work clothes. He carries his bowling jacket and a red-stained package from a butcher's. He stops at the foot of the steps to his apartment, hollers for his wife, heaves the package at her, then starts back around the corner. . . .*

BLANCHE *comes around the corner, carrying a valise. . . . She is daintily dressed in a white suit with a fluffy bodice, necklace and earrings of pearl, white gloves and hat, looking as if she were arriving at a summer tea or cocktail party in the garden district. She is about thirty. Her delicate beauty must avoid a strong light.*

Should I establish a season?

Whether they are described in the text or not, your character has thoughts, feelings, sensations, and ideas related to the time of year. Imagine now the differing sensations of stepping out on an icy winter's night, an autumn afternoon, a spring morning, a noontime summer day. Events are inextricably tied to specific seasons: fall classes, a June wedding, spring break, summer vacation. Seasons affect your well-being, for example, Guinevere (in Lerner and Loewe's *Camelot*) is itchy to flee the castle for the May woods, Ratso (in the film *Midnight Cowboy*) has succumbed to a freezing winter's virus, Shannon (in Williams's *Night of the Iguana*) is boiling from a bus ride in the Mexican tropics in September.

The season dictates what you wear and anticipate. Walk outside. How does the air hitting against your cheek make you feel? Oppressed or energized? What greenery do you see? Miles of lush forests or one barren tree? You will recoil if you walk out of your New York City apartment and it's 100 degrees in the dead of winter.

Note how the season affects Anne Frank stuck inside the attic in the following sequence from act 2, scene 2 of *The Diary of Anne Frank* by Frances Goodrich and Albert Hacket.

Thursday, the twentieth of April, nineteen forty-four. Invasion fever is mounting every day. Miep tells us that people outside talk of nothing else. For myself, life has become much more pleasant. I often go to Peter's room after supper. Oh, don't think I'm in love, because I'm not. But it does make life more bearable to have someone with whom you can exchange views. No more tonight. P.S. . . . I must be honest. I must confess that I actually live for the next meeting. (*Work light off.*) Is there anything lovelier than to sit under the skylight and feel the sun on your cheeks and have a darling boy in your arms?

How does weather affect clothes and behavior?

You are dressed now for the weather. Indoors, you adapt to chilly conditions by grabbing a coverlet, pulling on a sweater or warm slippers. Outside, you respond to rain, snow, sleet, sunlight, wind, lightning, thunder, fog, humidity. Onstage, weather conditions may erupt suddenly: thunder cracking, winds howling, lightning striking.

Weather intensifies action. For example, the blizzard in Horton Foote's *Tomorrow* heightens the actions of each character, and it makes the scene more exciting by adding suspense:

A young woman, black-haired, poorly dressed, thin, gaunt, almost emaciated, comes in R. She is pregnant. Her clothes are patched and worn and no protection at all against the cold. She gets as far as the boiler room, and she faints. FENTRY *starts outside to wash the dishes when he hears the woman moan in pain. He steps outside the door, and he goes over to her and gently rolls her over on her back. He sees how cold her thin arms and legs are and takes his coat off and puts it over her. He feels her pulse, watches her for a moment longer and then shaking her gently, he tries to rouse her.* Lady. Lady. (*She opens her eyes slowly.*)

How do I rehearse for weather?

To respond to a dripping rain, freezing wind, or broiling sun, imagine the weather condition, then work against its effect on your body. For example, for heat, you could recall the sensation of lukewarm perspiration beading up on your forehead, then wipe those beads with your fingertips. For snow, imagine thin flakes trickling down on the crown of your head; scrunch your shoulders forward to minimize saturation. Notice different places where a weather condition touches your body. For example, rain hits the nape of the neck and gives you a chill between the shoulder blades. As you try to overcome the sensation, you (and the audience) will begin feeling the rain.

Remember to adapt to the weather slackening or intensifying, because weather may dull interest if it is too consistent. Work a scene first without weather conditions, then add a mounting or lingering rain, wind, fog, snow, throughout the scene. Fabricate weather early on in rehearsal by incorporating technical effects (lights darkening or brightening, candles glowing, etc.) to work against.

Is the day of the scene significant?

Besides using the season and weather, many playwrights set a scene on a particular day, such as Christmas, New Year's Eve, a birthday, wedding, or reunion. *Ah, Wilderness!*, whose beach scene we have been studying, takes place at the climax of summer, the Fourth of July.

Smart actors emphasize the theatrical significance of the day. They know that actions that characters might ordinarily stomach repel them on special occasions like Thanksgiving Day. If someone begins cursing at your Thanksgiving dinner, an expectation for people to act lovingly will probably increase your distress.

Ask yourself, "Is this the first day of the week, a weekday, or a weekend?" Sometimes the day itself promotes a crisis onstage. Note how upset the family is because they can't figure out what day it is as they await the Nazis in their attic hideout in act 2, scene 4 of *The Diary of Anne Frank:*

Dussel: Something has happened, Mr. Frank. For three days now Miep hasn't been to see us! And today not a man has come to work. There hasn't been a sound in the building!

Mrs. Frank: Perhaps it's Sunday. We may have lost track of the days.

Mr. Van Daan: (*to* ANNE) You with the diary there. What day is it? (ANNE *closes the diary so he cannot read what she is writing.*)

Dussel: (*coming up to* MRS. FRANK) I don't lose track of the days. I know exactly what day it is! It's Friday, the fourth of

August, Friday, and not a man at work! (*He rushes down to* MR. FRANK *again, pleading with him, almost in tears*) I tell you Mr. Kraler's dead. That's the only explanation. He's dead and they've closed down the building, and Miep's trying to tell us!

Mr. Frank: She'd never telephone us.

Dussel: (*frantic, indicating ringing telephone*) Mr. Frank, answer that! I beg you, answer it!

Should I keep a journal?

Keeping a journal can help stimulate your imagination. Studies have shown that 80 percent of what you learn each day you forget. Note how the time of day affects you in real life. Watch the changing of the seasons, the way people adjust to weather, to light, how time influences even the way people breathe. By recording these observations, you broaden the sources for expanding your imagination.

How do I rehearse time passing?

One of the quickest ways to establish time passing is through change: a switch in clothing, hairdo, or behavior. For example, in scene 1, it's Saturday morning at the dormitory. You, a freshman, have been sleeping in your cut-off jeans because you were up most of the night. You start picking up pretzel bags and Coke cans scattered around the room. In scene 2, it is two years later in the same dormitory. You are dressed in a blue pinstripe suit, eating sliced fruit, and scanning the *Wall Street Journal*. The changes in your clothing, hairdo, and behavior reveal that time has passed since your freshman days. Recent advances in computerized lighting and sound effects can clarify subtleties of time onstage. For example, with lights you can create a palpable difference between dawn and 11 A.M. Sometimes you can add these technical elements in rehearsal to heighten your concentration.

EXERCISES

1. *Listing Activities.* Write out activities appropriate to 2 A.M. for Jim or Mother in this sequence from act 3, scene 1 of Arthur Miller's *All My Sons.* Jim, a friend of the family, is warning Mother to stop waiting up for her son. Stage the sequence.

Two o'clock the following morning, MOTHER *is discovered on the rise, rocking ceaselessly in a chair, staring at her thoughts. It is an intense, slight sort of rocking. A light shows from upstairs bedroom, lower floor windows being dark. The moon is strong and casts its bluish light.*

Presently JIM, *dressed in jacket and hat, appears from the Left, and seeing her, goes up beside her.*

Jim: Any news?

Mother: No news.

Jim: (*gently*) You can't sit up all night, dear, why don't you go to bed?

Mother: I'm waiting for Chris. Don't worry about me, Jim, I'm perfectly *all* right.

Jim: But it's almost two o'clock.

Mother: I can't sleep. (*Slight pause*) You had an emergency?

Jim: (*tiredly*) Somebody had a headache and thought he was dying. (*Slight pause*) Half of my patients are quite mad. Nobody realizes how many people are walking around loose, and they're cracked as coconuts. Money. Money-money-money money. You say it long enough it doesn't mean any-thing. (*She smiles, makes a silent laugh*) Oh, how I'd love to be around when that happens!

Mother: (*shakes her head*) You're so childish, Jim! Sometimes you are.

Jim: (*looks at her a moment*) Kate. (*Pause*) What happened?

Mother: I told you. He had an argument with Joe. Then he got in the car and drove away.

Jim: What kind of an argument?

Mother:	An argument, Joe . . . he was crying like a child, before.
Jim:	They argued about Ann?
Mother:	(*slight hesitation*) No, not Ann. Imagine? (*Indicates lighted window above*) She hasn't come out of that room since he left. All night in that room.

Note: The scene continues for several pages. For an extra incentive in class, try doing the *entire* scene.

2. *Passage of Time.* Stage a sequence involving your normal routine at a specific time. For example, you're returning home from work. Note your work dress. What routine items do you deal with—mail, the refrigerator, recorded phone messages?

Restage this sequence set two years later or at 4 A.M. Allow for change of hairdo, clothing, and behavior to reveal a different time.

3. *Social Context.* Biff and Happy Loman in Miller's *Death of a Salesman* are living in a society experiencing declining morality in post–World War II America. They are feeling mounting anxiety in personal issues, a queasy fear in relationships, a collapsing self-esteem, and the dissolution of family life. In class, discuss how the brothers are lost in their careers in the late 1940s and how their outlooks have changed from when they were boys.

4. *Clocking Time.* Observe how many rooms in your house have a clock or other timepiece. Jot down whenever you look at one over a twenty-four-hour period and why. Determine when you are most dependent on time.

What is urgency?

Go, sir, gallop, and don't forget that the world was made in six days. You can ask me for anything you like, except time.

Napoleon Bonaparte

Action onstage happens within a compact time frame. What your character is doing you must accomplish at this moment. Urgency heightens a scene's interest. The more important your action is to you, the more involved you will become in it. In fact, the audience's experience of time depends on your attitude toward your action. If you throw yourself wholeheartedly into what you are doing, time appears critical.

How do I rehearse for urgency?

Tardiness, hurrying, weather, time of day, holidays, work hours may all put pressure on your character. Are you so late that you must perform actions quickly? Do you need to concentrate to get this demanding action done? Does a holiday spirit fire you to try a difficult feat? Discover why you are under pressure each second.

Find your way of creating urgency from the outset. Imagine time pressuring the initial moments of each scene. For example, ask yourself in rehearsals, "Does my character want to be in this house? How long do I imagine this situation should last? Should I try to exit after entering or to leave early?"

To stimulate urgency, some actors imagine a time bomb concealed in their pockets, which will go off if they don't get what they want in a scene. Others stick to urgent tasks. A critical activity gives you some place to put your concentration, so if you don't buy what the other character is doing, you have the option of going back to your activity. Furthermore, your life can continue if that character never enters. Some actors like to rehearse using an urgent, independent activity from the outset of the scene. For example, you are writing a chapter that you have to finish in the next fifteen minutes. Your assistant is waiting to type it. She's going to lunch in a half-hour. But you have to deal with someone knocking at the door to ask something that has nothing to do with this.

Why is "time running out" important?

If you cannot determine the urgency of a scene, you can always add the element of time running out. For example, in *The Glass Menagerie*, Amanda corners her son for ten minutes before he goes to work at the warehouse. Their scene begins with the ringing of an alarm clock and continues with Amanda insisting that he continue to waste his youth in a dead-end job in order to provide for Laura. Similarly, in Peter Shaffer's *Amadeus*, Salieri desperately pleads for help as the clock winds down.

SCENE 2

Salieri's Apartment

November 1823. The small hours

Salieri: (*a clock outside in the street strikes three*) I can almost see you in your ranks—waiting for your turn to live. Ghosts of the Future! Be visible. I beg you. Be visible. Come to this dusty old room— this time, the smallest hours of dark November, eighteen hundred and twenty-three—and be my confessors! Will you not enter this place and stay with me till dawn? Just till dawn—merely six o'clock!

(*he peers hard at the audience, trying to see it*)

Now, won't you appear? I need you—desperately! This is the last hour of my life. Those about to die implore you! . . . What must I do to make you visible? Raise you up in the flesh to be my last, last audience?

To some degree, all characters struggle against time to get their needs met. Even in comedies, characters confront pressing situations. In the following sequence from James McLure's *Laundry and Bourbon*, note how Hattie makes a futile effort to control the chaos her children are causing at her mother's house.

Hattie: Figure I better check on the kids. No telling what devilment they've gotten up to. (*Dialing*) Everything gonna turn out fine you'll see. (*On the phone*) Hello? Cheryl? Cheryl dear, this is Mommy . . . Mommy . . . your mother. (*Aside*) Child needs a hearing aid. What's that dear? Vernon Jr. threw a rock at you? Well, throw one

back at him, honey. Show him who's boss. Cheryl, Sweetheart, put
Grandma on the phone . . . Cheryl this week! (*Pause*) Sounds like
they're running her ragged. Hello? Little Roger. Is that you. I don't
want to talk to you right now punkin, I want to talk to Grandma . . .
'cause I want to talk to Grandma . . . yes Grandma does have
baggy elbows. Now lemme talk to her . . . what's that? Honey of
course Mommy loves you . . . I love you all the same. . . . Do I love
you more than who? Fred Flintstone. Yes. More than Paul New-
man no, but Fred Flintstone yes. . . . It's a grown-up joke, Honey.
Now put Grandma on. . . . She's what? Tied up! You untie her you
hear me? You want a switchin'?

Time is the thief you cannot banish.

Phyllis McGinley, "Ballad of Lost Objects"

■ THE PLACE

What is place?

Place is the specific location (building, neighborhood, state,
country) of the action. What can be done to create an interesting place in a few months, weeks, even days of rehearsals? Begin by examining the play's set description. Some playwrights
detail each item. If the playwright does not localize a scene,
start posing questions. If you are playing a witch in *Macbeth*,
ask: "What is the layout of this open heath in Scotland? Do thunder and lightning provoke me?" and so forth.

Stage truth happens on a ground plan that is an arranged reality. Visualize the colors, shapes, textures, and the arrange-
ments suggested. Your stage designer may have made particular
interpretations of the writer's suggestions. After you understand the setting, and the purpose of its angles and colors, you
will automatically start to adapt to the place. If you establish a
particular neighborhood, a specific room with doors in it, with
ordinary exits, with characters coming and going, sitting at
tables, peering out windows, that place will influence the way
you interact.

How do I build on the floor plan?

Take time to create a well-laid-out space for a scene. Walk around the floor, adjusting movements, testing doors, lounging in furniture. To fill in a ground plan, look for what you are doing onstage besides talking. Stop, fantasize, build the space surrounding the action. Even when the space inhibits you, it provides expressive possibilities. You need to choose actions to overcome it. For example, the chilly beach at night—pebbles, brush, light beams—could hinder Muriel's dash down the shadowy path to meet Richard in act 4, scene 2 of *Ah, Wilderness!* If Richard is killing time, strolling, daydreaming, what objects might distract him—an old bottle, wrecked boat hull, cold puddle?

(RICHARD *starts to stroll around with exaggerated carelessness, turning his back on the path, hands in pockets, whistling with insouciance "Waiting at the Church."*)

(MURIEL MCCOMBER *enters from down the path, left front. She is fifteen, going on sixteen. She is a pretty girl with a plump, graceful little figure, fluffy, light brown hair, big naive wondering dark eyes, a round dimpled face, a melting drawly voice. Just now she is in a great thrilled state of timid adventurousness. She hesitates in the shadow at the foot of the path, waiting for* RICHARD *to see her; but he resolutely goes on whistling with back turned, and she has to call him.*)

A theatrical place furthers the conflict. Think of how theatrical the following situations might be: (1) to escape from a combat zone; (2) to sleep in a sewer; (3) to exercise in a china shop; (4) to laugh in a morgue; (5) to blow up a museum.

EXERCISES

1. *A Childhood Room.* Visit a room from your childhood and encounter, through each of your senses, its uniqueness. Record your impressions. In class, map out the room. Use chairs, tables, and other items available in the acting area.

Visualize furniture, objects, and their location for the audience. See if you begin to remember how you felt in that room at that time.

2. *Diagramming the Place.* Develop your own favorite romantic beach. Link the make-believe shoreline, sea, and path to actual landmarks onstage: crevices in the floor, objects, curtains, lights. With the other actor in the scene, draw an exact diagram of the stage floor. In laying out the floor plan for an outdoors scene at a beach, ask, "Where does the coastline run across the set? Do any trees create a pathway? From which direction does the tide gush in? Does it churn up the waves and sand or spray foam? Is a moon or sun beaming down from overhead?" List objects for rehearsal. Explore the entire ground plan, such as how items in a skiff, under a sand pile, behind driftwood can forward your action. Even on an empty beach, certain remaining items—a perfumed letter, some rotting fish, the springy sand, your busted hat, a ripped towel, a dirty bucket, a cracked bottle—could compel attention. Infecting the silence, they provoke your response.

3. *Time Running Out.* Choose a simple task in a familiar place, using objects related to your need and the obstacle of too little time.

■ OBJECTS

How do I find privacy onstage?

Acting with privacy means acting as if no one is watching you. When you are truly private onstage, you are relaxed and totally comfortable. You act as if no one is observing you, much as you do when you are alone, at home. In most scenes, you must discover what you do when you feel completely relaxed, comfortable, and unobserved. You find this privacy through associating the place with your own activities and things. Most important is your relationship to the objects around you onstage.

Learning how to use objects helps actors experience life on the stage, which is different from but analogous to real life. Dealing concretely with objects gives you a real sense of belief in the stage place. For example, an actress hung a portrait of her real-life father on the set when she played a father-dominated alcoholic.

Fabricate a believable environment for yourself through association with your personal objects. Imagine decorating your character's childhood room. Use objects from your own life: your books, sapphire marbles, rock albums. When you replace these for the final production, you will have experienced an investment in personal objects. Ask yourself, "What toys did I fight over? A shiny piggy bank, a one-eyed teddy bear? What childhood treasures, like racing car stickers, Christmas photos, college pennants, might kindle memories of my mother, father, and friends?"

Continue your exploration at rehearsal by roaming around the room. Claim your bed, your books. Suggest connections by asking, "What objects did I leave in my old room?" or "What room have I felt touched by in a movie or book that resembles this place?" or "What mementos do I long to take away with me?" Transforming the set into a place that you inhabit encourages interesting actions. Imagine activities you could engage in, such as "checking out the old room" or "getting ready for bed."

How should I endow props?

"To endow" means to deal with a false object as if it possesses real qualities. Imagine handling a ragged rug like a plush oriental, a bottle of water like an exotic perfume, an empty teakettle like a boiling one, a scrap of paper like an ardent love letter. Endowment is critical for hazardous objects onstage such as a razor blade, knife, and gun.

To endow false props with qualities they don't possess, use sense memory to recall the qualities of real things you own. Sense memory means remembering the physical sensation of objects. You can practice with your own real objects that have certain sensual qualities of touch, taste, smell, sight, sound. Then you act as if the stage prop has the same qualities by adjusting the way you handle it.

How do I practice endowing?

Practice endowing objects at home and in rehearsals. When you smell the salt breeze, your nose contracts in a certain way. Capturing that one adjustment can stimulate a whole series of unconscious thoughts and feelings. Note how one actor has jotted down certain physical sensations connected with the lines of the beach scene from *Ah, Wilderness!*

LINES	SENSE MEMORY (sight, hearing, touch, smell, taste)
RICHARD (*Thinking aloud*): Must be nearly nine.	What do I see to make me think it's nearly nine? Do I see my watch, the clock, feel the wind getting cooler?
I can hear the Town Hall clock strike,	Does the clock chime, gong, how far away is it? Am I counting chimes?
it's so still tonight.	What do I hear? A distant ship. Feel? No wind on my cheek.
Gee, I'll bet Ma had a fit when she found out I'd sneaked out.	Do I hear Mother calling "Richard"? See her checking my bed covers?
I'll catch hell when I get back, but it'll be worth it.	Do I feel Dad's belt strap? Taste having no dinner for two days?
She didn't say for certain she could . . . gosh, I wish she'd come! . . .	Should I grab the letter again? Should I hear her voice, feel the touch of her cheek?
Am I sure she wrote nine? . . .	Grab the letter.
(*He puts the straw hat on the seat amidships and pulls the folded letter out of his pocket and peers at it in the moonlight*)	What does the straw hat I bought to make an impression feel like after two hours on the beach? Damp, sandy? Do I rip at the straw?

Yes, it's nine, all right.
(*He starts to put the note back in his pocket, then stops and kisses it— then shoves it away hastily, sheepish, looking around him shamefacedly, as if afraid he were being observed*)

What does the crinkled letter smell like? Rose perfume? Do I reread it? How does it taste when I kiss it? Salty, musty from my pocket? Do I fondle it?

To improve his sense memory, this actor rehearsed the activities outdoors at night on an abandoned skiff. He also got ideas from observing pictures and films of lovers on the beach at night.

Why do all objects need an emotional life?

Some objects won't need physical endowment (for example, you may deal with a letter as a letter), but all objects need psychological endowment. Recall the way you handled a cherished teacup, your fashionable senior ring, or the bear-claw patchwork quilt Grandma sewed. If you spent your last twenty-five dollars on a bright blue picture book and then dropped it in the gutter, you would salvage it with gusto.

In one performance, when the maid said, "Oh, you dropped your book, Sir," the actor lost at least three moments because he just picked it up. Had he fully endowed this book, he might have played a moment where he dusted it off, checked it out, retrieved his place. You may think, "Maybe he didn't need those moments," but his cursory treatment of the book and other objects ultimately resulted in an unconvincing performance.

What is a fourth wall?

Most sets provide you with three walls. To complete your world you will need to imagine objects on a fourth wall behind the audience. Concoct a fourth wall containing points to focus on when you look out toward the audience. Facing forward is the most powerful position for the actor, but controlling concentration from this vantage point is the most difficult.

To control your focus, create the fourth wall as a part of the script's particular location. Identify on a fourth wall behind or between audience members five to seven places that you can spot from where you are positioned onstage. For instance, in a blackened auditorium, you may still spy (without seeing audience members) a red exit sign, a lighted aisle, a lacquered doorway.

If you are sharing the scene with other actors, determine your fourth wall together. Lay out together the same imaginary objects at certain spots on the fourth wall—a blue sailboat, a treacherous wharf, a leaning post. Take as much time to assign fictional objects to these spots as you would to arrange real stage furniture.

When working in an outdoors scene or on an arena stage, you must often create four walls surrounding you with objects of primary importance such as a little village with a few white steeples way down at the bottom of the hill, or crashing surf on the reef next to you. Explore your emotional relationship to these objects and to their distance from you.

What are a primary and a secondary fourth wall?

Using a primary fourth wall means dealing directly with something on that wall. For instance, you might point out something there, such as the moon. Pick a spot in the auditorium to look at; then adjust your body—especially head and shoulders—to the correct tilt they would have if the spot were miles away, like the moon. Similarly, if you're looking in a mirror five inches away, you might focus on the exit sign and adjust your body accordingly. Using a secondary fourth wall means dealing indirectly with the wall behind the audience. You rely on the wall as a backdrop. For example, as you read this, you are trusting a secondary fourth wall. Now look up and imagine talking to a friend. You will look at that person, but your eyes will also take in the fourth wall backdrop behind her. When you sit in the yard, you spontaneously include the fourth-wall view. You are not focusing on the fourth wall but are including its presence behind whatever you see. Trusting in your fourth wall helps you relax and perform freely, that is, act with privacy onstage.

EXERCISES

1. *Psychological Endowment.* Bring into class three important objects from your life. Talk about one of them. Don't prepare in advance what you are going to say. When you start talking, you should experience a real stream of consciousness inspired by the object.

2. *Physical Endowment.* Stage a scene in which you use three of the following objects. Endow each object with strong physical qualities, such as a *boiling* teakettle, *dripping* ice cream, *bitter* cough syrup:

shoe polish	mascara
teakettle	cough syrup
ice cubes	nail polish
razor	ice cream
gun	

3. *Psycho-Physical Endowment.* Restage the preceding exercise by endowing the same objects with psychological traits, such as a *magical* teakettle, *forbidden* ice cream, or *poisonous* cough syrup.

4. *Primary Fourth Wall.* Stage a monologue or scene in which you use the fourth wall in a primary way.

5. *Secondary Fourth Wall.* Stage a phone conversation in which you use the fourth wall in a secondary way. When you talk on the phone, allow yourself to automatically gaze at different spots on the fourth wall as you focus on the listener.

6. *Re-Create a Telephone Conversation.* Relate to the subject matter or content, not to the sound of the person's voice.

■ ATMOSPHERE

What is atmosphere?

After you have determined the floor and the walls of your scene, imagine what its atmosphere might be. "Atmosphere is the emotional sphere enveloping the space," wrote Michael Chekhov, Russian actor and disciple of Stanislavski, in *The Actor's Eye.*

Chekhov said that when you enter a place, certain elements around you—sounds, smells, sights, temperature conditions—stimulate your thoughts and feelings, and you react in a certain way. The atmosphere of the place excites your personal reaction. A vast cathedral with a grave atmosphere evokes pity from some but silence from others.

How people react to the same atmosphere may differ dramatically. Observe how the atmosphere around you right now evokes certain body sensations, thoughts, or feelings influencing your actions.

In real life, we are unconsciously affected by the rattling of the wind, the groaning of the sea, the tolling of chimes, the cawing of a lonely bird. We notice the bug on our sock, the rusted fishing pole, the seashell on the ground. A film actor, through the magic of a sound track or special effects, is sometimes able to hear the rustle of leaves, to battle real drafts piercing through a flimsy shack, or to feel rain dripping down from the skies. Onstage, you must use sense memory to fashion your own reactions to the elements of nature.

Besides physical elements, atmosphere embraces the emotional conditions attached to a place. You *can* sense the tranquility, sadness, emptiness in a room. When you enter a gloomy scene, you can feel the sorrow in the air. You often work against the atmosphere. When you see someone crying, you say, "Don't cry! Things will get better!"

How can I create atmosphere?

Creating atmosphere involves both experiencing something in the air and adjusting to that sensation. We do this automatically in life, so it will be easy to do onstage after you become aware of atmosphere's importance. First, get into the habit of noticing atmosphere. When you enter rooms, streets, buildings, conscientiously observe their atmosphere so you will notice dynamic ones. Next, study the creation of other atmospheres in art: in films, pictures, and books.

Stanislavski said that when standing before a painting, you should squeeze yourself into the frame of the painting in thought, try to enter into it, so as to become infected with its mood and become physically accustomed to it, not from without, but from within. When creating atmosphere for a particular scene, reread the script and imagine yourself inside its world, in that flea-bitten basement or marble palace. Use Stanislavski's "Magic If" phrase to grapple with those objects and people and unlock your particular responses. In rehearsal, experiment with moving in harmony with a particular atmosphere. For example, imagine a sadness in the air; observe what sensations and feelings arise. Or imagine the air permeated with smoke. How do you react to that? Because it's easier to envision the room loaded with smoke than with sorrow, next conceive sorrow as a real weight in the air that you work against.

EXERCISES

1. *Harmonious Atmosphere.* Move in harmony with the following atmospheres:

   fresh aroma of a florist shop

   uplifting air of a cathedral

   serious mood of a library

   cold air of a tomb

2. *Sorrowful Atmosphere.* Stage a serious sequence, then conceive sorrow as a weight in the air that you work against.

3. *Sweet Atmosphere.* Imagine yourself in the mountains of North Carolina in June. Breathe the crisp air, smell the sweet woods, sense the bright sky, feel the refreshing greenery.

4. *Your Present Atmosphere.* Close your eyes and allow yourself to experience the atmosphere around you right now. Then open your eyes and move harmoniously within it.

How do selected details create the space?

Developing your place is like redoing a room. You begin with the floors (ground plan), the walls (the fourth wall), objects (endowment). Then you move into more intangible areas—the atmosphere (feeling of a place). Add new elements after you have mastered old ones. An exciting place evolves from an infusion of details.

■ CHECKLIST

This checklist should help you explore exciting details in your place. Answering these few basic questions should encourage a vigorous response to the setting.

1. What is my emotional response to this setting?

2. What is the weather like?

3. What experiences have I had here or in a setting like this?

4. What am I dressed for? Why?

5. What must I do in this setting?

■ FINAL PROJECTS

A friendly reminder: There is no right or wrong way to do any of these exercises. Their purpose is to help you discover the influence of the setting on a scene. Let your teacher help you interpret them in the way most beneficial to you.

1. *Progressive Exercise.* **EXERCISE 3:**   A stalled train. Use the same partner from the previous progressive exercises. Two more years have passed, and your relationship has changed dramatically. Reveal time's passage for this scene through changes in clothing, hairdo, and behavior. A change in profession or health is always dramatic. It is now four years since you initially met in Progressive Exercise 1. Establish the day, season, and weather conditions. Re-create the time by outlining the events of the day. Establish the exact place, including the outdoor neighborhood and the world inside the train. Plan where you will place furniture and objects for certain activities.

   Now each of you should play an action that conflicts with the other. For example, one of you is studying, and the other is doing vocal exercises.

   Begin the sequence with each of you performing a task in silence, then one of you begins a conflict.

2. *Privacy.* Re-create one action in a place where you feel completely at ease, totally unobserved. Work with objects to experience the stage as a "real" setting. For example, you might make a salad in your kitchen at noon or get dressed in your bedroom at dawn. Your mounting involvement in the action should lessen your sense of being watched by the audience, so you act as if you are in private.

3. *Childhood Setting.* Create a vivid ground plan, fourth wall, and atmosphere for a short scene. Imagine re-creating objects from a similar room from your past, for example, the red plaid bed covers, tarnished trophies, rusted bar weights, scratched maple desk, deflated basketball, yellowed university catalogues for a boyhood room.

   Stage a conflict with two characters. Examine what you two might have done together in the past. Establish objects — phone, schoolbooks, and so on — that will help you create an exact time frame and an old routine together. Now decide on and perform a new routine in which your actions conflict. Stage the scene, re-creating these conditions and actions.

Optional: Put a small clock in your pocket, and set the alarm for one minute before you expect the sequence to end. Pretend the clock is a time bomb that will explode if you don't get what you want *right now* in the scene.

4. *Atmosphere.* Incorporate a tense atmosphere into a scene set in a bedroom. Close your eyes and remember a time when you were surrounded by an anxious atmosphere. You and another had repressed your feelings and a hostility existed between you. Relax your eye muscles behind your lids and imagine what you did at that time. Imagine in detail all the physical elements of that place from your own life, similar to the setting in a play. In rehearsal, each of you should walk around the stage and demonstrate these special elements to the other, then agree on certain ones and collaboratively re-create a sense of atmosphere. Hand in a detailed description of the place: ground plan and atmosphere. Stage the scene, if possible.

8
GIVEN CIRCUMSTANCES
What is my life situation?

This chapter evaluates how previous, present, and future events and conditions affect your character's actions.

Life cannot wait until the sciences may have explained the universe scientifically. We cannot put off living until we are ready. The most salient characteristic of life is its coerciveness: it is always urgent, "here and now," without any possible postponement. Life is fired at us point blank.

Jose Ortega y Gasset

■ WHAT ARE GIVEN CIRCUMSTANCES?

This expression means . . . the story of the play, the facts, events, epoch, time and place of action, conditions of life, the actors' and director's interpretation, the mise-en-scene, the production, the sets , the costumes, properties, lighting and sound effects— all the circumstances that are given to an actor to take into account as he creates his role. (*Stanislavski Handbook*, p. 67)

Your circumstances—previous, present, and future situations—control much of what you do. For example, your character, Pete, enters the stage. He is coming home from work after a fourteen-hour shift at the railroad. He is expecting to be embraced by his mother and sister. His mother has promised to cook him a marvelous roast, like she did for his birthday, and his sister should be practicing his favorite tune on the piano. These circumstances affect how you, as Pete, greet your mother (your first action upon entering).

Given circumstances are the physical, emotional, and social conditions spelled out by the playwright. You must connect with them emotionally and fill in the blanks in those circumstances that are implied. You must also find a framework of associations from your life to activate you onstage. After you begin anchoring your lines with these associations, you will find yourself having more commitment to even the smallest actions.

Circumstances can influence your conflicts, fuel your motivation, and shape your action. Our circumstances can never be studied enough.

How do I find my circumstances?

Picture an actor living in the year 2091 portraying you. What vital circumstances would she have to unjumble about you to interpret your actions? You would expect the actor to spend time observing your best photographs, studying your relationships at work, empathizing with the tensions, concerns, and issues permeating your home, understanding your circle of friends.

Similarly for any character you play you must search for clues. You can sensitize yourself to circumstances by looking at other plays. Similar tensions unite the works of many playwrights. Witness the strain between father and son in many of Arthur Miller's plays.

Study related works—recordings, films, books. If, for example, you are impersonating Lorraine Hansberry (the first black woman playwright to be produced on Broadway), listen to her taped interviews. If you are playing the voluptuous Marilyn Monroe type in Arthur Miller's *After the Fall*, investigate the many films of Monroe (Miller's ex-wife), the cult books on her, and the photographs. In the play itself, you must comb stage directions about time and place as well as dialogue and what's hidden under the words. You have to understand not only what happens in the play but also the circumstances under which it happens.

How do I evaluate the play for given circumstances?

Begin by examining the plot. Each play has its skeleton of events. Answer the question "Without what occurrences would there be no play?" Reread the play to experience the progression of circumstances. Jot down flashes of similar experiences from your life. A plot summary of *The Glass Menagerie* by Tennessee Williams reveals the key circumstances.

> Tom Wingfield, alternating in the roles of narrator and participant of the "memory play," evokes the home in St. Louis which he left years ago: the drab reality of the little flat in a dark alley; his monotonous job in a warehouse from which he escapes by writing poetry; his mother, a former Southern belle who tried to govern her two grown children by the constantly recalled standards of her girlhood; his sister Laura, a shy, slightly crippled girl who found refuge in the imaginary kingdom of her glass animal collection; and Jim, a friend from the warehouse whom Mother, determined to find a "gentleman caller" for her daughter, had forced Tom to invite, and who for a moment falls under the spell of Laura's dream world. Tom, too, flees from his mother and sister, but he cannot banish the thought of their fragile, helpless existence. The play has the delicate twilight atmosphere of time remembered, "truth in the pleasant disguise of an illusion." (from Van Cartmell, *Plot Summaries to 100 Plays*)

Substituting and particularizing circumstances are a key part of your work. You look at plot for the circumstances that change during each scene for the progression of circumstances and changes between scenery and acts. What are circumstances around your life at home, at work, on vacation, in love?

How do other characters' circumstances affect me?

You will learn much about your character's situation from observing the circumstances of the other characters. At a quiet time, jot down impressions of their predicaments from your character's perspective. Imagine playing Tom in *The Glass Menagerie*, set in the 1930s. Note how the same circumstances influence you and your mother, Amanda, differently. For example, she cheers and you regret having the Gentleman Caller to dinner.

THE GLASS MENAGERIE: CIRCUMSTANCES

CHARACTER	CRITICAL CIRCUMSTANCES
Father: (*absent*)	Charming ways, his records, postcards, picture, his love for long distance, and abandonment of the family
Jim: (*Gentleman Caller*)	Charming ways, his go-getter attitude, his money ethic, his love for dancing, his interest in sports, his "secret" engagement, his success at the warehouse, his concern about the future, his obsession with television, his scholarship, his failures after high school
Tom:	Thirst for adventure, the boredom in St. Louis, the tiny apartment without privacy, his cot in the living room, his obsession with writing, his disgust with the shoe warehouse, his drinking and movie watching, his attraction to the Merchant Marine, his function as the provider of the family
Amanda:	Her enormous girlhood popularity and social standing, her exaggerated storytelling, glamorizing past boyfriends, her money-success ethic, the limited opportunities for women in 1939, her total dependence on Tom, her previous attempts to get Laura a boyfriend, her fun at church socials and with her friends, her love for both children as her *whole* life, her abandonment by men
Laura:	Her peculiarities: her limp, her shyness, her withdrawal with glass toys, her love for Tom and her mother, her worship of Jim, her failure at high school and business school, her lying to her mother about typing, her visits to the penguins, her obsession with the Victrola and her father's old records

■ THE SCENE BREAKDOWN

What is a scene breakdown?

Fire up your imagination by doing a scene breakdown for circumstances, evaluating the play scene by scene for key conditions. Sometimes actors will note who's in the scene, the number of pages, location, key event. If the play is not broken down by the playwright into scenes, your director may do this and explain how she views the sequence of key scenes. Note how provocatively one actor has assessed circumstances by scene for *The Glass Menagerie*.

THE GLASS MENAGERIE: SCENE BREAKDOWN

This dream play flashes onto the stage a memory: Tom's recurring nightmare about saving his sister Laura from a complete breakdown. Each scene reveals Laura's inability to cope: make a living, marry, adapt in the real world. Each character tries to save Laura, but then physically or emotionally abandons her.

Scene Tag (Key Action, Emotional Experience)	Setting (Spot Creating Circumstance)	Characters (Others Experiencing Problems)
1. Saving the old maid (tragic and comic)	Fire escape landing Alley apartment interior	Tom, Amanda, Laura

A winter's evening in an alley apartment in St. Louis, where Amanda is urgently trying to teach her grown children manners, style, and the right attitude for a winning marriage. Amanda pretends that a caller could come any minute in the hopes of encouraging some responsiveness from Laura and Tom. Amanda acts as if she is still a belle on a plantation. Laura exposes her dread of being abandoned as an old maid, a state akin to starving in 1939.

2. Using the keyboard (tragic)	Interior	Amanda, Laura

Another freezing twilight. Laura pretends to practice typing, but Amanda, returning home from the business college, and not the D.A.R., reprimands Laura for never having attended her typing classes. Laura has been visiting penguins and tropical flowers in glass houses at the zoo. Laura reveals a secret high school crush, and Amanda, realizing a business career for Laura is impossible, desperately encourages her to cultivate charm to offset her crippled condition and attract a husband.

3. Attacking Tom   Fire escape   Tom, Amanda, Laura
    (tragic and comic)   Interior

An evening in late winter. Getting a gentleman caller has become an obsession for Amanda. Turning into a nagging witch, she attacks Tom for his moping, doping, and coming in late each night. Hurling his coat at her, he jars the glass menagerie where Laura, terrified, is observing them, then he flees.

4. Escaping the coffin   Fire escape   Tom, Laura
    (tragic and comic)   Interior

The next morning, 5 A.M. booms from a bell in a nearby church tower. Laura greets the drunken Tom and quiets him to bed. Laura experiences his desperation as Tom compares his plight as provider for her and Amanda to being alive in a nailed-up coffin.

(Three more scenes complete the play.)

How does a scene breakdown reveal circumstances?

A scene breakdown usually includes a scene tag, the setting, and the characters. A scene tag underscores the key action and serves as a reminder of where you will be focusing attention. For example, if the key action in scene 1 "Saving the Old Maid," is "warning Laura about old maidship," then you'll probably ask yourself, "Why was spinsterhood dreaded? What did it mean to be an unmarried woman in the 1930s? How would she survive? What would she do?"

The setting and characters of the scene signal your circumstances. Scene 1, "Saving the Old Maid," takes place on the fire escape and interior as Tom vacillates between abandoning his sister and remaining trapped in a two-room apartment. If you are playing Tom, you might speculate, "When have I gone outdoors and where to escape being trapped in an impossible situation at home? Have I ever lived in close quarters for any length of time? How did it make me feel?"

In scene 1, Amanda is concerned about Laura's spinster status. Why? Do you have someone in your family whom your mother is concerned about? What doom do you fear for this person? How do other relatives' outlooks about this person differ from yours? What tensions could develop because of different sensitivities over the same situation?

How can a scene breakdown help my acting?

An actor usually knows from the outset whether the play is a comedy or tragedy, but a study of the scene breakdown will clarify *how* it is comic or tragic. The circumstances in a comedy cause frustration and in a drama, sorrow. For example, if you couldn't get your sister to stop daydreaming, you might feel frustrated. But if you couldn't save your sister from a mental collapse, you would feel sad. The seriousness of the circumstances differs, but the frustrated character is as determined as the dramatic one about achieving his goals.

Although drama usually has a sad ending and comedy a happy one, many plays (even Shakespearean tragedies) contain funny as well as sad scenes. Depending on which circumstances you choose to support the scene, you will lean toward a comedic or a dramatic interpretation.

A scene breakdown can help your acting in smaller, more specific ways by illuminating details of your situation, which enrich your interpretation of each small piece of the scene.

How can I feel the part?

Now that you understand the given circumstances of the play, you will need to experience them. Begin by looking up key words in reference books. By opening up windows into the words, you prick your curiosity about what you want to do with them. An intriguing definition, an imperceptible shade of meaning, can reveal your character's thoughts.

For example, if you are playing a hysterical alcoholic, you could begin with the obvious dictionary definition of "alcoholic": "suffering from a diseased condition due to the excessive use of alcoholic beverages." You might then pursue a richer encyclopedia description. Books on human behavior can yield information about addiction. You piece together your character's alcoholism from a variety of sources: dictionaries, psychology books, medical books, and reference books.

What is the "Magic If"?

Imagination! Imagination! I put it first years ago, when I was asked what qualities I thought necessary for success upon the stage. Imagination, industry, and intelligence—the three I's—all indispensable to the actor, but of these three, the greatest is, without any doubt, imagination.

Ellen Terry, British actress, *The Story of My Life,* 1908

The "Magic If" is a method for surrendering yourself to the character's circumstances. Stanislavski said that you must imagine yourself as the character by using "if." If you were in the character's situation, and if you had the same needs and values, and if you made the same choices, you would become the person. Each of us has a vast subjective potential to be a nun, a murderer, a thief. To embrace these circumstances, use the "Magic If" as the starting point.

To use Stanislavski's "Magic If," say to yourself, "If I were the character in these circumstances, what would I do?" Using the "Magic If" helps actors step into the world of memory. You remember various experiences and imagine certain conditions, then you mentally put yourself there. For example, you picture a train wreck you saw in life or in a film, then you imagine yourself there. You sense how you might feel and act in that situation. You leap into the scene emotionally, through this mental connection of "what if."

Next, you picture yourself as the *character* in the circumstances. You imagine, "What if I were in a train wreck and I were an IBM executive, not myself, then what would I do?" You picture the lifestyle of that executive, and you fantasize how her actions might differ from yours in the scene. Use the "Magic

If" to expand your expressiveness as the character. When you mentally see yourself as the character in the circumstances, you discover exciting possibilities to experiment with. Appropriate action leaps to mind.

What is subtext?

Subtext is hidden information you use below the line to strengthen meaning. As you work on each scene, you'll find places where you'll need to fill in the blanks with specific associations. If you're playing Blanche in *A Streetcar Named Desire*, you will have to contact Blanche's feelings about teaching school. Determine when she taught, say, 8 A.M. to 3 P.M. (six sections of honors English)—and the hourly routine. Was she respected by her colleagues, admired by her students?

Because most characters are jolted awake by extreme circumstances, find those moments of trauma. Trauma—an injury, wound, mental shock—creates a violent collision in the mind. Observe the confrontation here, the juicy word there, and the deathlike pause somewhere else. Fill in these spaces with vivid subtext. Note the sore spots italicized in Blanche's opening scene in *Streetcar*.

A STREETCAR NAMED DESIRE: **BLANCHE'S SUBTEXT**

Eunice: I think she said *you taught school* [Trauma—I lost my job]

Blanche: Yes.

Eunice: And *you're from Mississippi,* huh? [Trauma—I got kicked out of there]

Blanche: Yes.

Eunice: She showed me a picture of your home-place, *the plantation.* [Trauma—I lost it]

Blanche: Belle Reve?

Eunice: *A great big place with white columns.*

Blanche: Yes . . .

Eunice:	A place like that must be *awful hard to keep up.* [Trauma—It's being demolished]
Blanche:	If you will excuse me, I'm just *about to drop.*

Any confrontation requires more unspoken information, or subtext, than dialogue. Words are like a veil. What lurks behind them out of sight, concealed, repressed, tinges the veil with significance. That mass of hidden experiences creates meaning onstage.

For example, you will have to evoke a stream of crises to activate Blanche's lines. Her bankruptcy, degeneracy, and her dependence on her only sister all pressurize her present action "to find a haven at her brother-in-law's cramped apartment."

Erotic memories, premonitions, fantasies flash beneath different lines. Expand on her impressions and phobias to support your stage action.

EXERCISES

1. *Associating Facts.* Jot down initial associations for the following facts about Blanche in *A Streetcar Named Desire.* Read the first three scenes of the play.

FACTS		ASSOCIATION
where you live	208 Esplanade	John's apartment
whether you are married	widow	breakup with John
whether you have children	_____	_____
whether you behave yourself	_____	_____
whether you are underpaid	_____	_____
whether you are disciplined	_____	_____

whether you are healthy	_____	_____
whether you are meticulous	_____	_____
whether you are aggressive	_____	_____
whether you are critical	_____	_____

2. *Theatrical Circumstances.* Imagine one day in the fantastic circumstances of a theatrical character. Write down observations. Do an exercise in class on how your character gets up in the morning.

3. *Current Circumstances.* In pairs, tell each other your worst current circumstances, for example, if you're broke, your mother is ill, you have just gotten divorced, or you have just been robbed. Note what associations pop into your head as you speak and listen.

What is "living the role"?

"Living the role" means providing yourself with a direct experience of the character's circumstances. Some actors go a great distance to do this. For example, if your character was raised on a plantation, you might spend a day at a plantation, read about leisure class life, see southern films. You could prime yourself to experience the thoughts, sentiments, and sensations of life there. Gradually, you will begin acquiring a sensitivity, a cognizance. Meryl Streep is reported to live the circumstances of the character outside rehearsals—reading, eating, doing only things her character would do.

More often, actors find indirect experiences to correspond with their characters' circumstances. They weave their own memories and fantasies into their characters' thoughts. Compelling actors associate every person, place, and thing their characters talk about with a personal experience.

What are previous circumstances?

Previous circumstances are anything that has happened recently to your character that affects you right now onstage. Jim, the Gentleman Caller in *The Glass Menagerie*, is lonely for his fiancée, so he flirts with Laura. Previous circumstances predispose you to pursue the character's action.

If you are playing Jim, find the circumstances that make you lead Laura on. Ask yourself, "In my life, what person so worshipped me that I encouraged her?" Did you approach her with disdain, with relish, with tension? What were the circumstances? She lived next door, was friendly with your younger sister, used to watch you play baseball, grinned at you. Contact your own past so that Jim's past affects your present actions.

Experiencing previous circumstances can help you expand the expressiveness of your initial actions. Practice what happened before your character enters. For example, if you have been traveling all night from one grimy bus station to the next, your legs will feel cramped as you enter. Experiment with the slowness of your gait. How might your shoulders slump from hauling heavy luggage? Try dragging luggage onstage. Work on the previous circumstances for the first moment. If you are specific and believable, you are laying the groundwork for the truth of the scene to evolve naturally.

What are present circumstances?

Present circumstances are conditions hitting you as you enter the stage. Look for physically expressive choices that can be read by the audience. For example, if your character has been stuck with a busload of complaining women in 100-degree Mexico, you might drag yourself into the hotel, you might wipe your brow as you say hello to the hotel manager. Or you might gulp down some water, unbutton your shirt, remove your hat, and dry the inner hatband. You do specific things to make that heat real for yourself. If you can capture the truth of one circumstance—you really feel hot (and adjust to that heat) as you enter—that will stimulate truth in other parts of the scene.

Consider during the rehearsal process what you can convey to the audience. To give your character dramatic bite, rehearse active information, such as your back hurts, your feet are sweating, you are fighting a stuffy nose. Test a range of choices to find the most active. Sometimes after performing a rather flat scene, actors will say, "If you only knew the story I made up—" and I'll respond, "Look, if it doesn't come across in your actions, you won't have a chance to get up there and explain." When acting goes well, you affect the audience with the same emotions that you are undergoing. Physical choices clarify what you are experiencing and immediately trigger audience response.

What are future circumstances?

Onstage, there are two types of future circumstances: the real (what actually will occur) and the expected (what the characters imagine). Expectation—the fiction that your character imagines—is what you play. You long for the opposite of what appears. Interweave expectations, the mental pictures, thoughts, and conditions you want with your character's actions.

For each scene, ask yourself, "What positive future might I imagine?" Expectations are vital to a riveting performance. Each moment you are actually working for something you don't get. Train your imagination to expect the improbable! When you are constantly surprised by what occurs, your expectations are working.

1. *Investigating Circumstances.* Underline all circumstances you would need to experience if playing a character in one of the following scenes.

Oscar Wilde, *The Importance of Being Earnest,* Act 1

(LADY BRACKNELL *and* ALGERNON *go into the music room;* GWENDOLEN *remains behind*)

Jack:	Charming day it has been, Miss Fairfax.
Gwendolen:	Pray don't talk to me about the weather, Mr. Worthing. Whenever people talk to me about the weather, I always feel quite certain that they mean something else. And that makes me so nervous.
Jack:	I do mean something else.
Gwendolen:	I thought so. In fact, I am never wrong.
Jack:	And I would like to be allowed to take advantage of Lady Bracknell's temporary absence . . .
Gwendolen:	I would certainly advise you to do so. Mamma has a way of coming back suddenly into a room that I have often had to speak to her about.
Jack:	(*nervously*) Miss Fairfax, ever since I met you I have admired you more than any girl . . . I have ever met since . . . I met you.
Gwendolen:	Yes, I am quite aware of that fact. And I often wish that in public, at any rate, you had been more demonstrative. For me you have always had an irresistible fascination. Even before I met you I was far from indifferent to you. (JACK *looks at her in amazement*) We live, as I hope you know, Mr. Worthing, in an age of ideals. The fact is constantly mentioned in the more expensive monthly magazines, and has reached the provincial pulpits, I am told; and my ideal has always been to love someone of the name of Ernest. There is something in that name that inspires absolute confidence. The moment Algernon first mentioned to me that he had a friend called Ernest, I knew I was destined to love you.
Jack:	You really love me, Gwendolen?
Gwendolen:	Passionately!

Eugene O'Neill, Ah, Wilderness!, *Act 3, Scene 2*

SCENE—*Same as Act I—Sitting-room of the Miller home—about 11 o'clock the same night.*

MILLER *is sitting in his favorite rocking-chair at left of table, front. He has discarded collar and tie, coat and shoes, and wears an old, worn, brown dressing-gown and disreputable-looking carpet slippers. He has his reading specs on and is running over items in a newspaper. But his mind is plainly preoccupied and worried, and he is not paying much attention to what he reads.*

MRS. MILLER *sits by the table at right, front. She also has on her specs. A sewing basket is on her lap and she is trying hard to keep her attention fixed on the doily she is doing. But, as in the case of her husband, but much more apparently, her mind is preoccupied, and she is obviously on tenterhooks of nervous uneasiness.*

LILY *is sitting in the armchair by the table at rear, facing right. She is pretending to read a novel, but her attention wanders, too, and her expression is sad, although now it has lost all its bitterness and become submissive and resigned again.*

MILDRED *sits at the desk at right, front, writing two words over and over again, stopping each time to survey the result critically, biting her tongue, intensely concentrated on her work.*

TOMMY *sits on the sofa at left, front. He has had a hard day and is terribly sleepy but will not acknowledge it. His eyes blink shut on him, his head begins to nod, but he isn't giving up, and every time he senses any of the family glancing in his direction, he goads himself into a bright-eyed wakefulness.*

Mildred: (*finally surveys the two words she has been writing and is satisfied with them*) There. (*She takes the paper over to her mother*) Look, Ma. I've been practicing a new way of writing my name. Don't look at the others, only the last one. Don't you think it's the real goods?

Mrs. Miller: (*pulled out of her preoccupation*) Don't talk that horrible slang. It's bad enough for boys, but for a young girl supposed to have manners—my goodness, when I was your age; if my mother'd ever heard me—

Mildred: Well, don't you think it's nice, then?

Mrs. Miller: (*sinks back into preoccupation—scanning the paper vaguely*) Yes, very nice, Mildred—very nice, indeed. (*Hands the paper back mechanically*)

Mildred:	(*is a little piqued, but smiles*) Absent-minded! I don't believe you even saw it. (*She passes around the table to show her* AUNT LILY. MILLER *gives an uneasy glance at his wife and then, as if afraid of meeting her eye, looks quickly back at his paper again.*)
Mrs. Miller:	(*staring before her—sighs worriedly*) Oh, I do wish Richard would come home!
Miller:	There now, Essie. He'll be in any minute now. Don't worry about him.
Mrs. Miller:	But I do worry about him!

2. *Associating Memories.* Close your eyes, relax your eyelids, and imagine the circumstances your character is experiencing in the first exercise. Remember a time when you were worried about a proposal or waiting for a missing relative, then stage the *Earnest* or the *Wilderness* sequence.

3. *Physicalizing Circumstances.* Communicate one of the following circumstances through what you do physically. Your suitcases are heavy. You are tired, your clothes are dirty. You are freezing, your hair is falling out. You are broke.

4. *Worst Circumstances.* Describe to another character the worst circumstances you have experienced. Remember how they made you feel; for example, terrified in a bank holdup, cautious in a job interview, cowardly at a traffic accident.

How can I tell whether my circumstances are effective?

Consider whether the circumstances lead you to the most dramatic choice. A French production of *The Winter's Tale* by Shakespeare immediately visualized the agony of Paulina. The actress playing Paulina, when discovering her queen's death, acted with abandon. Bending over at the waist, she tossed her long black hair like a mask over her face. Then she encircled the king as she yelled curses at him for killing his queen. When on the edge of despair, individuals often dare extreme choices.

Onstage, highlight the astonishing aspects of your character's circumstances. Imagine yourself in a fantasy or dream. Riveting choices like those in a dream inspire the audience to greater self-knowledge. "Nowadays more and more people, especially those who live in large cities, suffer from a terrible emptiness and boredom, as if they're waiting for something that never comes," Jung wrote in *Man and His Symbols*. "Movies and television, spectator sports, and political excitements may divert them for a while, but sooner or later they have to again face the tedium of their everyday lives."

To enter the "dream," the actor allows herself to be completely driven by circumstances through a series of occurrences. Even the tiniest circumstance seethes with significance. The actor must completely trust the other characters and audience to succumb to an almost selfless experience. The actor expands beyond the self and truly becomes someone else.

■ BACKGROUND

How does background affect your circumstances?

Background triggers your circumstances. The more you can experience the predicament of your character, the more you'll respond intuitively each moment. Fill in the blanks about the character's world so that you can react impulsively. You can never know too much background. Your character's background directly affects your feelings about each situation.

How do I write background?

The following backgrounds show areas to be evaluated to excite your impulses. A student actor wrote this character sketch as homework, although he spent some time in class determining which facts (such as setting, circumstances) were common to his character and his scene partner's. Whenever possible, these questions should be answered for every scene you do.

Note how the background connects with the overall action, "to stall Nancy," so she can get a cheaper room. Whether improvised or scripted, dramatic action must be supported by this sensory framework. These elements are the center of any role. Incorporate them early on, and you're on your way to an exciting performance!

1. Who am I? (Chapter 6: Character)

I am Kit. I am twenty-four years old. I live in New Orleans and work as an accountant for an import/export business that is going bankrupt. My professional handicap is that I am meticulous about saving money. This obsession has escalated into a sickness.

I was born in Pascagoula, Mississippi. Rumor is my mother was knocked up at Keesler Air Force Base, and then my dad split the scene. My mother died when I was two. I was raised in a foster home by her distant cousin, a widow with three daughters. I mowed grass, worked as a waiter, and then as a bookkeeper to put myself through public college. I am determined never to be poor and dependent. My wizardry with accounting landed me a fabulous job with an export company, but . . . [This biography can be fleshed out further.]

2. Where am I? (Chapter 7: Setting)

I am with Nancy in the waiting room, sixth floor, west wing of the chic Laurel Canyon General Hospital near Beverly Hills, California, U.S.A. What is around me?

There are mauve chairs, a table neatly stacked with *Baby* and *Glamour* magazines, ashtrays, a dispenser of mineral water, and a big plant. Over the intercom system, doctors' names are being paged. It smells sterile and sweaty at the same time. I am unfamiliar with the place, since I have never been to this hospital before.

What time is it? November 23, 1990, 4 P.M., a sunny and bright California afternoon. It is four years since I first met Nancy. We are in the media/machine generation of videocassettes, calculators, films, air travel, high-tech finance. Computer science, communications, and business (once considered trade fields) are dominant majors on college campuses. George Bush, sidekick to "ex-movie star" Reagan, is president. My hometown, New Orleans, is undergoing a severe economic depression. Hospitals are going bankrupt.

3. What are my circumstances? Past, present, and future events (Chapter 8: Given Circumstances)

I live in New Orleans with my wife, who has gotten help and been sober for a year. My dearest friend, Nancy, whom I met in Audubon Park four years ago, moved to California to escape her parents, got married to her therapist, and is now pregnant. Her husband, John, on a three-day assignment, has asked me to come to California to be with Nancy in case she goes into labor. Though he paid my way to California for his own comfort, I feel obligated to save him money. I am totally obsessed!

Nancy is getting tired of me. She was hoping for pampering and fun, but I have been obsessed with saving money, so much so that I went grocery shopping and bought generic food items. She is rich and doesn't need me to do this. I feel guilty because I was excited to come to California, when I am only supposed to be here for Nancy's benefit. Instead of allowing myself fun, I am punishing myself by trying to save John money.

I want Nancy to stay in the waiting room because there are only private rooms available costing almost twice the daily rate of double rooms. If Nancy goes into one, she would pay over $1,437.75 for the first two hours. Since she would probably end up staying in that room, escalating the cost, I am not paying attention to Nancy's labor pains, although her contractions are getting closer together. I have to go back home to my job in two days. John, Nancy's husband, will be back tomorrow.

4. What am I doing? (Chapter 1: Action)

Main Objective: To stall Nancy
Immediate Objective: To calculate savings
  What are the steps to this action?
  Silent activity: I am calculating from a figure table how much it would save John if we could wait until a double room is available in two hours. By waiting here for two hours it will save them $778.56. And, overall, for the duration of the stay, depending on the days (one day in double occupancy is $1,587.56, two days $3,175.12, and three days $4,762.68), a week would save almost $10,000 (if there are any complications like Down syndrome, incubation, fetal heart murmur, jaundice, or surgical procedures the stay could be longer).

Whereas for an improvisation you fabricate the most interesting facts, for scripted material you must enliven facts in the text. As you read through a script, note in pencil information about the following questions:

1. Who am I? (character)

2. Where am I? (setting)

3. What are my circumstances? (circumstances)

4. What is my action? (action)

SAMPLE BACKGROUND FOR SCRIPTED SCENE

Role: Martha in Edward Albee's Who's Afraid of Virginia Woolf?

1. Character

What way do I speak and move? What part of New England am I from? Is my parents' mother tongue English or German, French, Russian? Do I speak with a mixed melody pattern because of having lived different places before my father became college president? Did my father, the college president, use certain slang expressions? Do I imitate these? Did I pick up certain gestures from a peer group, especially around puberty? What are my major traits?

How can I fill in the following facts with memories, sensations from my life? (Note substitutions in parentheses.)

I was born fifty years ago tomorrow, the only daughter of wealthy, highly educated parents (my mom went to Radcliffe). My dad, a renowned college president, gave me the best private education (St. Martin's Episcopal), including four years at Wellesley (Wellesley alumni house). Ever since earliest childhood, I have been the little star (applause of teachers) at faculty parties (dinners on the Cape). As an only child (visits to Grandma's), I was often lonely and played with make-believe friends such as a pet mouse (my dog Brownie). Later I began drinking (college football weekends). I married right out of college (hot sex) and hoped to have four sons—all college presidents. I have no children (two miscarriages). [Biography needs to continue, expanding on details indicated in the script.]

2. Setting

What is my feeling about this living room? When did we buy this house? Why do we live on the campus of a small New England college? Where did I get certain objects, the old bookcase, the sofa, Daddy's picture, the liquor chest? How does this history professor's house differ from my childhood home as the college president's daughter?

How does the fact the play moves from 2 A.M. Sunday until dawn affect the rowdiness and final slowdown of my actions? How do I feel about the first faculty party of this year?

3. Circumstances

How did I meet George? What did we do together? What's the basis of our fascinating persecution of each other? More important, am I obsessed with my father? Why is my mother never mentioned?

What did I consume at the party we're returning from? Whom did I long to see or not see there? What was featured in the college paper today? Why do I do the following: pick up new faculty, insult my husband, stumble home drunk from a party, set up seduction scenes, enjoy lewd dancing, discuss my "son's" birth, plan impromptu cocktail parties, and disguise my barrenness?

■ FINAL REMARKS

I am the very slave of circumstances and impulse—borne away with every breath.

Lord Byron, *Sardanapalus,* act 1, scene 2

What is the perfect role?

Many actors search for the "perfect role" that fits like a glove with their own circumstances. But you should strive to play a number of roles and spend a lot of time on varied circumstances. Any transformation, like the development of a butterfly from a

cocoon, involves many minuscule adjustments. Daily altera-
tions (in rehearsal and in study at home) help you expand your
body and mind into the character's. The extent of that meta-
morphosis depends on your talent as well as your commitment
to research and practice and to justification of everything your
character says and does.

What is living the part?

The Stanislavski system is based on living the part, as he explained so clearly to his students.

> The art of living a part asserts that the main factor in any form
> of creativeness is the life of a human spirit, that of the actor and
> his part, their joint feelings and subconscious creation. . . . What
> we hold in highest regard are impressions made on our emo-
> tions, which leave a lifelong mark and transform actions into
> real, living beings. . . . Aside from the fact that it opens up ave-
> nues for inspiration, living a part helps the artist to carry out one
> of his main objectives. His job is not to present merely the ex-
> ternal life of his character. He must fit his own human quali-
> ties to the life of the other person, and pour into it all of his own
> soul. . . . An artist takes the best that is in him and carries it over
> on the stage. The form will vary according to the necessities of
> the play, but the human emotions of the artist will remain alive,
> and they cannot be replaced by anything else.
>
> Therefore, no matter how much you act, how many parts you
> take, you should never allow yourself any exception to the rule
> of using your own feelings.
>
> Salvini said: "The great actor . . . should feel the thing he is
> portraying . . . not only once or twice while he is studying his
> part, but to a greater or lesser degree every time he plays it, no
> matter whether is the first or thousandth time."
>
> Always act in your own person. . . . You can never get away
> from yourself. The moment you lose yourself on the stage marks
> the departure from truly living your part and the beginning of ex-
> aggerated, false acting.
>
> Spiritual realism, trust of artistic feelings . . . these are the
> most difficult achievements of our art, they require long, ardu-
> ous inner preparation.

The difference between this art and that practiced by others is the difference between "seeming" and "being." (*Stanislavski Handbook*, pp. 90–91)

■ CHECKLIST

The following checklist highlights how circumstances imbue the role with weight and meaning.

1. How does each line of the play affect my character?
2. How do I feel about my previous, present, and future circumstances?
3. What key events affect my character onstage?
4. What experiences can I associate with these events?

■ FINAL PROJECTS

1. *Progressive Exercise.* This exercise builds on the three previous progressive exercises. Use strong circumstances to anchor your action as the character.

   EXERCISE 4:   A hospital waiting room. Use the same partner from the previous progressive exercises. You are the same characters, but two more years have now passed. (Be sure to incorporate different hairdos, costumes, and behavior.) You may elect to use a handicap if you like. You have developed another type of intense relationship. You have shared many experiences.

   Together work out a scene in a hospital waiting room that is loaded with circumstances for you both. Each of you enters the stage with a troubling circumstance that never comes up in the scene. Although the circumstance bothers you, you never mention it. It simply adds weight to your character. Each of you does a task in silence for two minutes. Then one of you begins a conflict between you.

2. *Dramatizing Hello/Goodbye.* Pick a play and a character. Describe the play's principal sequence of events and your character's attitude toward each event. Rehearse a sequence in the play two ways: realistically and dreamlike. Stage the most compelling version for the class.

3. *The Offstage Event.* Choose a play in which a pivotal off-stage event dramatically influences a character's action. Do an improvisation on that encounter, then present it in class. For example, in *The Cherry Orchard* by Anton Chekhov, the offstage auction of the orchard affects the final departure scene of brother and sister.

4. *Similar Circumstances.* Choose a character with circumstances like your own. Research everything that is said about the character's circumstances in the play. Compare carefully all the information given by other characters. Note whether you feel they are reliable or lying. Answer "What are my circumstances?" in the most powerful way for your character. Hand in your research. Then stage a sequence from the play.

5. *Final Progressive Exercise.* Write a complete background for a final progressive exercise. This might also be considered a very structured improvisation.

EXERCISE 5: An empty cafe or restaurant. With the same partner from Progressive Exercises 1–4, you are the same characters, but two more years have now passed and you have further developed your relationship. (Be sure to include different hairdos, costumes, and behavior.)

Pick an empty cafe or restaurant that is loaded in atmosphere for you both. Include the features of time running out and an inner problem that never comes up in the scene. (The problem troubles you periodically and adds weight to your character.) With this inner problem, each of you begins an action in silence, then one of you starts a conflict between you.

The new factor in this exercise is that two couples are involved, and this scene has two beats (see page 2). The sequence begins with the two couples separated and a conflict occurring in each group. Then, at some point, a conflict erupts between the two groups. Remember, it is now eight years since your original appearance in Progressive Exercise 1.

Appendix A

■ IMPROVISATIONS, GAMES, EXERCISES

- Objects on a tray, p. 7
- Grocery store, p. 7
- Number shoot, p. 7
- Unrelated activity, p. 8
- My secret, p. 25
- Farewell, p. 33
- Emergency room, p. 33
- Crawling babies, p. 34
- Touch me, p. 34
- Repetitious exercise, p. 35
- Silent task, p. 35
- Improvising relationships, p. 35
- A complete relationship, p. 35
- Total conflict, p. 38
- Handicap walk, p. 56
- Physical obstacle list, p. 56
- Physical obstacle sequence, p. 56
- Problem computer, p. 56
- Blindfolded breakfast, p. 57
- Hardheaded monologue, p. 59
- Lost object, p. 60
- Recitation, p. 70
- Recalling events, p. 70
- The entrance, p. 70
- Crisis monologue, p. 70
- Inner problem, p. 70
- Sense memory, p. 73
- Emotional memory, p. 74
- Singing Shakespeare, p. 74
- Score your beats, p. 95
- The stranger, p. 99
- My style, p. 99
- Professional procedure, p. 99
- Character description, p. 99
- Physical trait, p. 104
- Imaginary garment, p. 104
- Different uniforms, p. 105
- Blindman's bluff, p. 105
- Physical condition, p. 105
- Character tasks, p. 105
- Fairy tale, p. 108
- Total war, p. 108
- Giant exercise, p. 109
- Mirror exercise, p. 109
- Calling qualities, p. 109
- Emphasizing traits, p. 109
- The bouncing ball, p. 109
- Character action, p. 109
- Character improvisation, p. 110
- Yearly diary, p. 115
- Treasured object, p. 115
- Life scripts, p. 115
- An interview, p. 119
- Collage, p. 119
- Clocking time, p. 132
- A childhood room, p. 136
- Diagramming the place, p. 137
- Time running out, p. 137
- Psychological endowment, p. 142
- Physical endowment, p. 142
- Psycho-physical endowment, p. 142

- Primary fourth wall, p. 142
- Secondary fourth wall, p. 142
- Harmonious atmosphere, p. 144
- Sorrowful atmosphere, p. 144
- Your present atmosphere, p. 144
- Privacy, p. 146
- Childhood setting, p. 146
- Theatrical circumstances, p. 159
- Current circumstances, p. 159
- Associating memories, p. 164
- Physicalizing circumstances, p. 164
- Worst circumstances, p. 164

Appendix B

■ KEY TERMS

- Beat, p. 2
- Psycho-physical action, p. 4
- Physicalize, p. 5
- Physical task, p. 6
- Stamina, p. 7
- Main action, p. 11
- Line-by-line actions, p. 13
- Build of a scene, p. 14
- Improvisation, p. 15
- Structured improvisation, p. 16
- Intention, p. 21
- Active verbs, p. 24
- Anticipation, p. 26
- Relationships, p. 31
- Personalizing relationships, p. 31
- Physical relationship, p. 32
- Psychological relationship, p. 32
- Responsiveness, p. 33
- Open scene, p. 38
- Major obstacle, p. 45
- Physical obstacle, p. 48
- Psychological obstacle, p. 52
- Vulnerability, p. 56
- Difficult obstacle, p. 57
- Relaxation, p. 65
- Inner monologue, p. 66
- Sense memory, p. 67
- Super objective, p. 77
- Major objective, p. 78
- Line-by-line objectives, p. 79
- Through line or spine, p. 81
- Prompt book, p. 85
- Becoming the character, p. 97
- Observation, p. 98
- Character analysis, p. 99
- Physical traits, p. 100
- Handicap, p. 102
- Professional traits, p. 103
- Animal traits, p. 103
- Machine traits, p. 104
- Imaginary garment, p. 104
- Psychological traits, p. 105
- Playing games, p. 108
- History, p. 110
- Life script, p. 113
- Journal, p. 130
- Urgency, p. 132
- Time running out, p. 134
- Floor plan, p. 136
- Privacy, p. 137
- Endowment, p. 138
- Physical endowment, p. 140
- Psychological endowment, p. 140
- Fourth wall, p. 140
- Primary fourth wall, p. 141
- Secondary fourth wall, p. 141
- Atmosphere, p. 143
- Scene breakdown, p. 153
- Feeling the part, p. 155
- "Magic If", p. 156
- Subtext, p. 157

- Living the role, p. 159
- Previous circumstances, p. 160
- Future circumstances, p. 161
- Background, p. 165

Appendix C

■ SCENE SELECTIONS

Man-Woman Scenes

All My Sons—Arthur Miller

Another Part of the Forest—Lillian Hellman

The Autumn Garden—Lillian Hellman

Barefoot in the Park—Neil Simon

Blithe Spirit—Noel Coward

Butterflies Are Free—Leonard Gershe

Cat on a Hot Tin Roof—Tennessee Williams

Cloud Nine—Caryl Churchill

Come Blow Your Horn—Neil Simon

A Coupla White Chicks Sitting Around Talking—John Ford Noonan

The Crucible—Arthur Miller

The Day They Shot John Lennon—James McLure

Driving Miss Daisy—Alfred Uhry

Epitaph for George Dillon—John Osborne and Anthony Creighton

Fool for Love—Sam Shepard

Forty Carats—Pierre Barillet and Jean Pierre Gredy

The Fourposter—Jan de Hartog

The Glass Menagerie—Tennessee Williams

Golden Boy—Clifford Odets

The Graduate—Calder Willingham

Here We Are—Dorothy Parker

I Am a Camera—John Van Druten

Joe Egg—Peter Nichols

La Ronde—Arthur Schnitzler

Last of the Red-Hot Lovers—Neil Simon

Loose Ends—Michael Weller

Lovers and Other Strangers—Renee Taylor and Joseph Bologna

Luv—Murray Schisgal

Mary, Mary—Jean Kerr

Our Town—Thornton Wilder

Period of Adjustment—Tennessee Williams

Picnic—William Inge

Plaza Suite—Neil Simon

The Prime of Miss Jean Brodie—Jay Presson Allen

The Prisoner of Second Avenue—Neil Simon

A Raisin in the Sun—Lorraine Hansberry

Ring Round the Moon—Jean Anouilh

The Rose Tattoo—Tennessee Williams

A Streetcar Named Desire—Tennessee Williams

Suddenly Last Summer—
Tennessee Williams
Summer and Smoke—
Tennessee Williams
Summertree—Ron Cowen
Sweet Bird of Youth—
Tennessee Williams
This Property Is Condemned—
Tennessee Williams
The Three Sisters—Anton
Chekhov
The Tiger—Murray Schisgal
The Time of Your Life—William
Saroyan
Tomorrow—Horton Foote
The Traveling Lady—Horton
Foote
Two for the Seesaw—William
Gibson
The Typists—Murray Schisgal
Uncle Vanya—Anton Chekhov
A View from the Bridge—
Arthur Miller
*Who's Afraid of Virginia
Woolf?*—Edward Albee

Woman-Woman Scenes

Agnes of God—John Pielmeier
All My Sons—Arthur Miller
Amphitryon 88—Jean
Giraudoux
*And Miss Reardon Drinks a
Little*—Paul Zindel
And a Nightingale Sang—C. P.
Taylor
Any Wednesday—Muriel Resnik
Bell, Book and Candle—John
Van Druten

Blithe Spirit—Noel Coward
Butterflies Are Free—Leonard
Gershe
Cactus Flower—Abe Burrows
The Chalk Garden—Enid
Bagnold
The Children's Hour—Lillian
Hellman
Cloud Nine—Caryl Churchill
Crimes of the Heart—Beth
Henley
The Dining Room—A. R.
Gurney, Jr.
*The Effect of Gamma
Rays . . .*—Paul Zindel
The Gingerbread Lady—Neil
Simon
The Glass Menagerie—
Tennessee Williams
Isn't It Romantic?—Wendy
Wasserstein
Joe Egg—Peter Nichols
Key Exchange—Kevin Wade
Laundry and Bourbon—James
McLure
Light Up the Sky—Moss Hart
Look Back in Anger—John
Osborne
Middle of the Night—Paddy
Chayevsky
The Miracle Worker—William
Gibson
The Miss Firecracker Contest—
Beth Henley
My Sister Eileen—Joseph
Fields and Jerome Chodorov
Night of the Iguana—
Tennessee Williams
Picnic—William Inge

The Prime of Miss Jean Brodie—Jay Presson Allen
Separate Tables—Terence Rattigan
The Skin of Our Teeth—Thornton Wilder
Steel Magnolias—Robert Harling
A Streetcar Named Desire—Tennessee Williams
Toys in the Attic—Lillian Hellman
Vanities—Jack Heifner
A View from the Bridge—Arthur Miller
A Young Lady of Property—Horton Foote

Man-Man Scenes

Ah, Wilderness!—Eugene O'Neill
All My Sons—Arthur Miller
All the Way Home—Tad Mosel
Another Part of the Forest—Lillian Hellman
The Bald Soprano—Eugene Ionesco
Biloxi Blues—Neil Simon
Brighton Beach Memoirs—Neil Simon
Buried Child—Sam Shepard
Come Blow Your Horn—Neil Simon
Death of a Salesman—Arthur Miller
The Dining Room—A. R. Gurney, Jr.

Driving Miss Daisy—Alfred Uhry
Equus—Peter Shaffer
Father's Day—Oliver Hailey
Feiffer's People—Jules Feiffer
Fifth of July—Lanford Wilson
The Glass Menagerie—Tennessee Williams
Glengarry Glen Ross—David Mamet
A Hatful of Rain—Michael Gazzo
Key Exchange—Kevin Wade
Lone Star—James McLure
Long Day's Journey into Night—Eugene O'Neill
Look Homeward, Angel—Ketti Frings
The Man with the Flower in His Mouth—Luigi Pirandello
The Master Builder—Henrik Ibsen
M. Butterfly—David Henry Hwang
The Odd Couple—Neil Simon
Period of Adjustment—Tennessee Williams
Precious Sons—George Furth
Private Wars—James McLure
Relatively Speaking—Alan Ayckbourn
A Soldier's Play—Charles Fuller
Streamers—David Rabe
That Championship Season—Jason Miller
True West—Sam Shepard
A View from the Bridge—Arthur Miller

Waiting for Godot—Samuel
   Beckett
We Bombed in New Haven—
   Joseph Heller
*Who's Afraid of Virginia
   Woolf?*—Edward Albee

The Widow Claire—Horton
   Foote
The Zoo Story—Edward Albee

Appendix D

■ MONOLOGUE SELECTIONS

Women

Butterflies Are Free—Leonard Gershe

A Chorus Line—Michael Bennett

The Country Girl—Clifford Odets

A Delicate Balance—Edward Albee

The Diary of Anne Frank—Frances Goodrich and Albert Hackett

Dream Girl—Elmer Rice

The Effect of Gamma Rays . . .—Paul Zindel

For Colored Girls Who Have Considered Suicide When the Rainbow Is Enough—Ntozake Shange

Fool for Love—Sam Shephard

The Gingerbread Lady—Neil Simon

House of Blue Leaves—John Guare

Isn't It Romantic?—Wendy Wasserstein

Kennedy's Children—Robert Patrick

The Lady of Larkspur Lotion—Tennessee Williams

Laundry and Bourbon—James McLure

Ludlow Fair—Lanford Wilson

Luv—Murray Schisgal

The Matchmaker—Thornton Wilder

Ma Rainey's Black Bottom—Augiust Wilson

'Night, Mother—Marsha Norman

Oleanna—David Mamet

Orpheus Descending—Tennessee Williams

Our Town—Thornton Wilder

The Philadelphia Story—Philip Barry

Plaza Suite—Neil Simon

The Sign in Sidney Brustein's Window—Lorraine Hansberry

Sister Mary Ignatius Explains It All for You—Christopher Durang

The Skin of Our Teeth—Thornton Wilder

Spring Dance—Horton Foote

The Star-Spangled Girl—Neil Simon

Steel Magnolias—Robert Harling

A Streetcar Named Desire—Tennessee Williams

Suddenly Last Summer—Tennessee Williams

Summertree—Ron Cowen

To Be Young, Gifted, and Black—Lorraine Hansberry
Two for the Seesaw—William Gibson
Vanities—Jack Heifner

Men

The Actor's Nightmare—Christopher Durang
Ah, Wilderness!—Eugene O'Neill
All My Sons—Arthur Miller
Amadeus—Peter Shaffer
The Boor—Anton Chekhov
Butterflies Are Free—Leonard Gershe
A Chorus Line—Michael Bennett
Come Blow Your Horn—Neil Simon
Dream Girl—Elmer Rice
Epitaph for George Dillon—John Osborne and Anthony Creighton
Equus—Peter Shaffer
Fool for Love—Sam Shepard
The Gingerbread Lady—Neil Simon
The Glass Menagerie—Tennessee Williams
House of Blue Leaves—John Guare
House Party—Ed Bullins
I Am a Camera—John Van Druten

Joe Egg—Peter Nichols
Long Day's Journey into Night—Eugene O'Neill
Look Homeward, Angel—Ketti Frings
Luv—Murray Schisgal
Mass Appeal—Bill C. Davis
Master Harold and the Boys—Athol Fugard
Moon for the Misbegotten—Eugene O'Neill
Oleanna—David Mamet
The Prisoner of Second Avenue—Neil Simon
The Proposal—Anton Chekhov
A Raisin in the Sun—Lorraine Hansberry
The Rimers of Eldritch—Lanford Wilson
The River Niger—Joseph A. Walker
The Seven-Year Itch—George Axelrod
Talley's Folly—Lanford Wilson
That Championship Season—Jason Miller
A Thousand Clowns—Herb Gardner
Tobacco Road—Erskine Caldwell
Two for the Seesaw—William Gibson
Uncle Vanya—Anton Chekhov
The Zoo Story—Edward Albee

Reading List

This brief list is offered as a starting point for those seeking further reading on the theater and acting.

Consult your library for additional suggestions.

■ ACTORS AND ACTING

Barton, Margaret. *Garrick*. 1949. Reprint 1978. An account of the life of one of the greatest actors, responsible for a radical change in the style of English acting in the eighteenth century.

Bernhardt, Sarah. *The Art of the Theatre*. 1924. Reprint 1969. The French personality actress sums up her career and her technique.

Chaliapin, Feodor. *Man and Mask: Forty Years in the Life of a Singer*. 1932. *Chaliapin, an Autobiography*, as told to Maxim Gorky. 1969. Autobiographies of the great Russian bass (1873–1938), known for his excellent acting as much as for his magnificent singing.

Courtney, Marguerite. *Laurette*. 1955. Reprint 1968. Biography of Laurette Taylor, who first appeared on the stage as a child, took the world by storm in *Peg O' My Heart* in 1912, and returned in 1945 to triumph again in *The Glass Menagerie;* by her daughter.

French, Yvonne. *Mrs. Siddons: Tragic Actress*. 1936. Reprint 1981. Main events in the life of this great English tragic actress (1755–1831), stressing her illustrious career and her brilliant technique.

Hillebrand, Harold Newcomb. *Edmund Kean*. 1933. Reprint 1967. A judicious life story of the great English tragedian (1787–1833): gives details of Kean's roles from contemporary criticism and commentary.

Macready, W. C. *The Journal of William Charles Macready, 1832–1851*. Abridged and edited by J. C. Trewin. 1967. The editor's notes give background to the great tragedian's diary entries.

Richardson, Joanna. *Rachel*. 1956. Portrait of one of the greatest actresses France, or perhaps the world, has ever known, seen in her nineteenth-century setting.

Salvini, Tommaso. *Leaves from the Autobiography of Tommaso Salvini*. 1893. Reprint 1971. Memoirs of the great Italian tragedian whose performance as Othello inspired Stanislavski to search for a universal law of creativity.

Stanislavski, Constantin. *An Actor Prepares.* 1936. Translated by Elizabeth Reynolds Hapgood. Sets down the concepts of sensory recall, emotion, memory, relaxation, concentration units and objectives, super objectives, communion, adaptation, and through line of action.

Stanislavski, Constantin. *An Actor's Handbook.* 1963. Edited and translated by Elizabeth Reynolds Hapgood. Describes alphabetically the key principles of the Stanislavski system.

Stanislavski, Constantin. *My Life in Art.* Translated by J. J. Robbins. 1924. Reprinted 1956. Tells of his career in the theater, and how he came to develop his system.

Weaver, William. *Duse: A Biography.* 1984. The life of Eleonora Duse (1859–1924), Italian acting genius, who rose from a poor itinerant acting family to be a great international actress. Notes, bibliography, and index add much to the usefulness of the book.

Young, Stark. *Theatre Practice.* 1926. Mostly on acting, with final chapter on Duse.

■ CRITICISM

Clurman, Harold. *Lies Like Truth: Theatre Reviews and Essays.* 1958. *The Naked Image: Observations on the Modern Theatre.* 1966. *The Divine Pastime: Theatre Essays.* 1974. Wise and discerning essays by the late director and critic.

Craig, Gordon. *On the Art of the Theatre.* 1911. Reprint 1925, 1958. Dissatisfied with the acting of his time, this designer-director wrote, "Today they impersonate and interpret; tomorrow they must represent and interpret; and the third day they must create." *Towards a New Theatre: Forty Designs for Stage Scenes, with Critical Notes by the Inventor.* 1913. Reprint 1968.

Hazlitt, William. *The Characters of Shakespeare's Plays.* 1817. Reprint 1962. *Hazlitt on Theatre.* 1895, as volume 2 of *Dramatic Essays.* Reprint 1957. Selections from *A View of the English Stage* and other essays on the theater and actors.

Jones, Robert Edmond. *The Dramatic Imagination: Reflections and Speculations on the Art of the Theatre.* 1941. The great designer presents an aesthetics of theater.

Lewes, George Henry. *On Actors and the Art of Acting.* 1875. Reprint 1957. This nineteenth-century English critic understood acting as few other critics of that or any other period have.

Shaw, George Bernard. *Play and Players: Essays on the Theatre.* 1952. *Dramatic Criticism: A Selection.* 1959. Shaw was drama critic for the *Saturday Review* from January 1895 to May 1898. His weekly writings in that capacity were collected in three volumes as *Our Theatres in the Nineties* (1932). Prior to the publication of this set, which is available and highly recommended, a selection had been edited by Huneker under the title *Dramatic Opinions and Essays.*

Young, Stark. *The Theatre.* 1927. Reprint 1958, 1980. *Immortal Shadows: A Book of Dramatic Criticism.* 1948. *The Flower in Drama, and Glamour: Theatre Essays and Criticism.* 1955. Stark Young, great American critic and practical man of the theater, has written about acting with more perception than almost any other.

■ THE DANCE

Cohen, Selma Jeanne, comp. *Dance as a Theatre Art; Source Readings in Dance History from 1581 to the Present.* 1974. An overall view of the history of theatrical dance in Europe and America. Theoretical essays, librettos, and excerpts from technical manuals combine with Cohen's introductions and headnotes to give the first adequate coverage of the subject.

De Mille, Agnes. *Dance to the Piper.* 1952. Autobiographical volume by the American dancer and choreographer whose dances for *Oklahoma!* revolutionized musical theater.

Graham, Martha. "God's Athlete," in Karl Leabo, ed. *Martha Graham.* 1961. Also in *This I Believe,* edited by Edward R. Murrow (1954).

Horst, Louis. *Pre-Classic Dance Forms.* 1937. Reprint 1987. Descriptions of court dances of the early sixteenth century, prior to ballet.

Leatherman, Le Roy. *Martha Graham: Portrait of the Lady as an Artist.* Photographs by Martha Swope. 1967. Text covers her entire career up to 1965; photographs, only her late work.

Morgan, Barbara. *Martha Graham: Sixteen Dances in Photographs.* 1941. Reprint 1980.

■ THEATER HISTORY

General

Brockett, Oscar Gross. *History of the Theatre.* 1968. 4th ed., 1981. A freshly written and illustrated story of the theater from the Egyptian passion play to "happenings" and other recent developments. Controversial new theories as well as long-accepted facts are presented.

Southern, Richard. *The Seven Ages of the Theatre.* 1961. World theater is presented by phases instead of time periods or countries. Theater history in different periods or countries shows a surprising similarity in phases.

Special Place or Time

Clurman, Harold. *The Fervent Years: The Story of the Group Theatre and the Thirties.* 1945. Reprint 1957. New ed. 1975. An account of one of the most vital theater organizations of the period.

Crowley, Alice Lewisohn. *The Neighborhood Playhouse: Leaves from a Theatre Scrapbook.* 1959. The story of one producing theater (1915–1927) that, growing out of the dramatic program of a settlement house, helped to bring the American theater to its maturity.

■ CREDITS

Chapter 1

From *My Life in Art* by Constantin Stanislavski.

Chapter 2

Chapter 3

440 Park Avenue South, New York, NY 10016. No nonprofessional performance of the play may be given without obtaining, in advance, the written permission of Dramatists Play Service, Inc., and paying the requisite fee. Inquiries concerning all other rights should be addressed to Dramatists Play Service, Inc.

From *The Man with the Flower in His Mouth* by Luigi Pirandello in *Pirandelo's One-Act Plays* by William Murray. Copyright © 1970 by William Murray. Reprinted by permission of Samuel French, Inc.

Chapter 4

Reprinted with permission of Joseph Warfield, actor, director, teacher.

Reprinted from *Building a Character* by Constantin Stanislavski.

Chapter 5

From *An Actor's Handbook* by Constantin Stanislavski. Copyright © 1963. Reproduced by permission of Routledge, Inc., part of the Taylor & Francis Group.

Suddenly Last Summer by Tennessee Williams. Copyright © 1958 by Tennessee Williams. Published by New Directions Publishing Corporation.

Ah, Wilderness!. Copyright 1933 and renewed in 1960 by widow of author, Carlotta Monterey O'Neill, from *The Plays of Eugene O'Neill* by Eugene O'Neill. Used by permission of Random House, Inc.

From *The Glass Menagerie* by Tennessee Williams. Published by Random House, Inc.

From *Plaza Suite* by Neil Simon. Copyright © 1969 by Neil Simon.

Chapter 6

Reprinted with permission of Dan Strickler.

A Long Day's Journey into Night by Eugene O'Neill. Published by Yale University Press.

From *An Actor's Handbook* by Constantin Stanislavski. Copyright © 1963. Reproduced by permission of Routledge, Inc., part of the Taylor & Francis Group.

Man and His Symbols, Aldus Books, 1964 by Carl G. Jung, ed. Permission granted by the J. G. Ferguson Publishing Company.

"The Neurotic Process as the Focus of Physiological and Psychoanalytical Research," by L. S. Kubie as cited in *I'm OK, You're OK*, by Eric Berne.

A Layman's Guide to Psychiatry and Psychoanalysis. Copyright 1947, 1957, 1968 by Eric Berne.

Chapter 7

From *The Diary of Anne Frank*. Copyright © 1956, renewed by Albert Hackett, David Huntoon, and Frances Neuwrith in 1986. Used by permission of Flora Roberts, Inc.

From William Faulkner's "Tomorrow." Published by Harold Ober Associates, Inc.

From *Amadeus* by Peter Shaffer. Copyright © 1980, 1981 by Peter Shaffer. Published by HarperCollins, Inc.

Laundry and Bourbon by James McLure. Copyright © 1982, James McLure. Professionals and amateurs are hereby warned that *Laundry and Bourbon* is subject to a royalty. It is fully protected under the copyright laws of the United States of America, and of all countries covered by the International Copyright Union (including the Dominion of Canada and the rest of the British Commonwealth), and of all countries covered by the Pan-American Copyright Convention and the Universal Copyright Convention, and all countries with which the United States has reciprocal copyright relations. All rights, including professional, amateur, motion picture, recitation, lecturing, public reading, radio broadcasting, television, video or sound taping, all other forms of mechanical or electronic reproductions such as information storage and retrieval systems and photocopying and the rights of translation into foreign languages, are strictly reserved. All inquiries should be addressed to Mary Harden at: Harden-Curtis Associates, 850 Seventh Avenue, Suite 405, New York, NY 10019.

From *Respect for Acting* by Uta Hagen with Haskel Frankel. Copyright © 1973 by Uta Hagen.

Chapter 8

From *Plot Summaries to 100 Plays* by Van Cartmell. Copyright © 1945 by Doubleday.

A Streetcar Named Desire by Tennessee Williams. Copyright © 1947 by Tennessee Williams.